WAIT,
WHERE AM I IN THIS?

WAIT, WHERE AM I IN THIS?

DR. LEE LONG, EDD, LPC-S

Trewe Talu House

Cover Designer : Jill Pickering
Book Interior Designer : Alice Briggs

ISBN (Paperback): 978-1-963366-08-2

Printed in The United States

Published by:
Trewe Talu House
(A Division of Novus Press Works)
https://www.novuspressworks.com/
Nashville, TN

To my wife Charlotte and our three amazing kids, Ella, Molly, and Rhodes - you are the best part of my life.

CONTENTS

FOREWORD

WAIT, Where Am I In This, written by Dr. Lee R. Long, is a brilliant book describing the path to self-actualization and to a sensitive reciprocal relationship with the other person. The proposal is essentially a new approach to an interpersonal model of relationship with a substantial emphasis on beginning with oneself. As the author writes, "relationship begins with ME." Dr. Long illustrates with unusual clarity how to focus on oneself in every situational experience and then shows how to connect easily with other people. He also reminds his readers that learning to trust oneself in each situation is important (i.e. have confidence in what I want/don't want as well as in my feelings and impulses for action); this is a crucial key starting point for opening the door for genuine interpersonal relationships.

I have worked with, written publications with, supervised and trained professionals in psychotherapy with the author for almost a decade. During the period I have known Dr. Long, he has embraced a dream of teaching the *lay public*, not his professional colleagues or other clinical-academic types, how to authentically and interpersonally engage one another. His dream has come to fruition with the publication of *WAIT, Where Am I In This*. In reading the book, I found it to be engrossing and easy to read. I'll use a phrase here often ascribed to other books—this book is "a page turner." Encountering Dr. Long's book was exciting because he presents innumerable examples illustrating his major points to clarify the path to self-actualization and interpersonal engagement. His personal examples make the words come alive as well as make them highly applicable.

Being an effective psychotherapist and CEO for several decades at a large clinical site in Fort Worth, Dr. Long is sensitive to learning issues, particularly those that apply to persons trying to modify their own behavior. He writes extensively of the difficulties of examining one's personal habits in reacting to various situations involving others. These situations range from raising children, and interacting with friends and work colleagues. Here again, this is where his many personal examples are so useful as they facilitate reader understanding.

Personal change is frightening and the author wisely assists the reader to move beyond the fear and to begin the personal process of self-renewal while taking small steps. Dr. Long addresses instances where failure occurs (the old patterns predominate) and encourages the reader to learn from their mistakes and to not give up on the change-process. Repeatedly, the reader is reminded that "what really matters is what matters to ME, not the other person!" This simple motto is critical to Long's path of self-actualization. "Practice, practice, practice" is the author's repeated encouragement.

Summarily, learning to live by one's preferences and not those of others is the ultimate goal. It is important to note that the author's proposals do not lead to a self-centered or self-indulgent lifestyle. Why? Because making genuine contact with the other person is always the second step of Long's path. The path results in an individual who is highly sensitive to others. And importantly, the path, in teaching one to concentrate on what "my personal preferences are," often results reciprocally in the other person revealing what they want.

This pathway is a never-ending process of learning. Over time, individuals learn to increasingly focus on the experience of themselves in situations as they interact with others who no longer control one's standards or expectations. Learners may not always get what they want, but the other person always knows where they stand as well as what they want.

Finally, it must be said that this book has nudged Interpersonal Theory into deeper waters as Dr. Long's path advocates an *interpersonal lifestyle* that begins with ME and NOT with just a description of dyadic activity and exchanges. Self-maturity and genuine interpersonal encounter require that an individual must first know their own "personal space /boundaries" (that is, where their preferences begin and end); and then, and only then, can the person establish a connection with another human being which is richly satisfying to both parties.

James P. McCullough, PhD.
Clinical Psychologist, Author and
Founder of the CBASP Therapy Model

DEAR READER,

I want to introduce you to an extraordinary character.

Someone whose voice may have been too quiet for too long. Someone whose brilliance may have been dimmed by doubt, criticism, or failure. Someone whose gifts to this world may have been given hesitantly, if at all.

I'm talking about you.

Yes, you—the person holding this book, perhaps standing in a bookstore right now, wondering if these pages are worth your time and money. (They are, I promise.)

In my three decades as a therapist, I've had the overwhelming privilege of witnessing thousands of people discover their authentic selves. I've seen what happens when we lay down the defenses we have built to silence our inner critics, when we stop trying to please others and we step fully into who we truly are. The transformation is nothing short of extraordinary.

But I'll be honest with you: This adventure is not easy. There will be moments when you will want to retreat into the comfortable familiarity of how you have always shown up. Moments when the vulnerability feels too raw, when the opinions of others seem too important, when the old stories about yourself feel too true to question.

For many who have gone before you and agreed to learning "Where Am I in This?", the adventure has not been without pain. But the individuals and couples who have taken the risk have later said it was worth every difficult step. Because looking for how others want you to show up for them or failing to understand how you impact others—both issues leave you drained. Drained from being in a place you are not sure you belong.

Here's the amazing surprise that awaits you: You may discover that the most enjoyable thing on the planet is just being who you are!

This book isn't about becoming a "better" version of yourself. It's about becoming the most authentic version—which, paradoxically, often means unbecoming all the things you thought you were supposed to be.

In the ancient story of Creation in the Christian faith, there are two characters, Adam and Eve. In the Garden of Eden they are told to stay away from one particular tree: the tree of the knowledge of good and evil. When that boundary is violated, an interaction with God ensues.

God's first question to the couple? "Adam, where are you?"

This is not a location question. It is a call to introspect.

Other questions are asked, like: "Who told you these things?" and "Did you do what I asked you not to?"

But that first question, "Where are you…in this…moment?" This is the question that will shape the rest of the pages of this book.

Adam, and Eve, for that matter, answer with a defensive, externalized response: "It was that woman YOU made," and "It was that serpent YOU made." All externalization and blame.

Through the years, this has been a distinct theme I have seen as I meet with people —and let me be honest, in my own life as well! It is easier to blame and look outside of ourselves rather than to learn "Where am I in this?"

Learning where you are—what you think, feel, experience and believe—helps bring clarity as to why you are where you find yourself.

Some hear these words and think, Is this self-care all about being self-indulgent? The quick answer to this is, No! Self-indulgence overlooks you. It is an attempt to make pain, hurt, and sorrow go away. It is not a look at where you are in the midst of those feelings. It is avoidance.

This adventure is not about indulgences but about gaining an understanding of where you are in the moments of life. The good, the bad, the ugly. It is about learning your starting point. Knowing where you begin and how to move, on your map of life, to the place you would like to be.

This is to be done without demanding the environment change for you. That demand is too costly to you. Why? Because you do not have control over the environment. You only have influence.

Learning to answer the question "Where am I in this?" creates a different response to the world around you.

Fair warning: People in your life may not always celebrate this evolution. We humans tend to resist change, even positive change in those we love. Your authenticity might make others uncomfortable, as it holds up a mirror to their own unexamined lives. Please do not let that deter your adventure. That's part of the process.

I wrote this book because I believe, with every fiber of my being, that the world desperately needs to understand where we are. We need to learn how to access the authentic you, not the carefully curated version. We need your unique perspective, your particular gifts, your specific voice. There are conversations that won't happen, ideas that won't emerge, and connections that won't form if you continue to hide.

Consider this your formal introduction to the adventure of being the most authentic version of yourself. The most important relationship you'll ever have. The most fascinating character you'll ever know. The most valuable person you've been overlooking.

Turn the page. With hope and belief in yourself, let the adventure begin!

P.S. All the stories in this book have been changed to protect confidentiality. Any resemblance to real people is purely coincidental (except for my stories—those are real, though my wife might argue with my version of events).

NOTE: Learning theory suggests that it takes several tries before a lesson "sticks." This being said, some of the concepts in the book may seem repetitive. They are. That's by design for this very reason.

THE QUESTION: WHERE AM I IN THIS?

CHAPTER 1

FINDING YOU AGAIN

LOOK AT YOU. No, really look. When was the last time you saw yourself—not through someone else's eyes, not as a reflection of what others need—really saw yourself?

Most of us have gotten so good at scanning others' reactions, anticipating others' needs, and adapting to others' expectations that we've lost sight of ourselves. Our every feeling, choice, and reaction has become tied to someone else's behavior.

Rachel sat in my office, a file folder of grievances clutched in her hands like a shield. Across from her, Tom's shoulders curved inward as if bracing for impact. Rachel was at a nine-point-nine on the divorce scale: one toe still in the marriage, the rest of her already out the door. Tom thought they were at a two.

"He gambles online. Plays too many video games. He's emotionally unavailable. He doesn't prioritize me." The words tumbled out of Rachel, precise and practiced. Each accusation landed like a dart.

Most people do one of two things when under attack: become defensive or collapse into self-flagellation. Tom was a self-flagellator.

"You're right," he said, tears welling. "I'm terrible. I'm the worst husband ever."

I held up my hand. "Stop. Both of you."

The room went quiet.

"Rachel, I want to teach you something about intrapersonal awareness—that's self-awareness. Right now, you're focused entirely out there"—I gestured between them—"on the interpersonal battlefield. But I don't know where you are in all of this. And if I don't know where you are, I can't know where the 'me' that makes up part of the 'we' begins. Without that, how can we possibly understand where your relationship stands?"

Confusion flickered across her face.

I tried again. "Talk to me about you."

"I'm hurt," she said. "I feel overlooked. Like he doesn't care about me."

"That's still about him. Stay with you. What's happening inside you?"

"Well…" She shifted in her seat. "I don't feel cared for."

"Keep going."

"I feel like I don't matter. Especially when he—"

"Stop right there." I leaned forward. "'I don't matter.' Stay with that. Why is it that every time we get close to the truth of how you feel, you immediately swing back to talking about Tom?"

Her eyes welled up, but these tears were different—deeper, rawer. "Because it's so painful to feel like I don't matter."

And there it was: the internal truth she'd been running from by cataloging Tom's failures. The pain of feeling like she didn't matter was so intense that she'd rather live in the safer territory of his shortcomings than step into the burning ground of her own hurt.

Rachel was having her first moment of coming home to herself. "I don't want to feel this," she whispered.

"I know," I said gently. "But feeling it is the only way through it. And you don't have to do it alone."

Tom, who had been quiet, spoke up. "I hear you saying you don't matter. To me, you matter more than anything."

"That's kind," I said, "but right now, this isn't about whether she matters to you. It's about whether she matters to herself. Rachel, are you willing to sit with that?"

She nodded slowly, the folder of grievances lying temporarily forgotten in her lap. Sometimes, the hardest path isn't the one between two people; it's the one that leads us back to ourselves.

Think of your inner world like a house. Some of us spend our lives as critics of everyone else's homes: pointing out their cracked foundations, judging their paint choices, tutting at their overgrown lawns. Meanwhile, we haven't set foot in our own living room in years. The dust has gathered, the pipes are creaking, and we don't notice because we're too busy peering through other people's windows.

What I want Rachel and all of the people I work with to realize is that you first have to understand the "me" in the relationship before you can understand the "we" of the relationship. Think of it like this: There's your intrapersonal awareness, how you understand yourself. Then there's your interpersonal awareness, how you show up in relationship to others.

Too often, we try to jump straight to the interpersonal part. We focus on how others see us, react to us, treat us, before we've even figured out how we see ourselves.

But if you don't know where you are, how can you know where "we" begins? You have to understand yourself—your needs, your values, your boundaries—before you can authentically show up in any relationship, before you can understand who you are in relation to others.

When both people do this work—when both the "me's" that make up a "we" are grounded in self-awareness—you can build something real. It's not about merging into one unit or losing yourself in another person. It's about two whole people knowing and being known, each bringing their full, authentic selves to the table to create a relationship that is more than the sum of their parts.

Every relationship in your life, whether it's with a partner, friend, family member, or the barista at your local coffee shop, is shaped by how well you know your inner world. It's like having an internal compass that either points true north or spins wildly depending on who's standing next to you.

Take Heather, for instance. She grew up in a home where emotions were treated like multiple choice tests: There was only one right answer, and it was whatever her parents were feeling. If her emotional reality didn't match theirs, she was wrong. She learned to abandon her inner home and live as a permanent guest in everyone else's.

Now she's in her thirties, successful on paper but spiritually homeless. From the outside, everything looks picture-perfect: great career, beautiful house, wide circle of friends. But inside? She's been fumbling in the dark so long she's forgotten what it feels like to see clearly.

Here's the thing about your inner world—sometimes you don't notice it's getting darker until someone flips on a switch. For Heather, that moment came on her birthday.

She sat in my office, twisting a tissue between her fingers. "I don't know what's wrong with me," she said. "Christina's been my best friend for years. We've been through everything together. But lately, every time I'm around her, I just feel...uncomfortable."

"Tell me more about that," I said.

"It's little things. She'll ask me to watch her kids, which I love doing. But when I need help, there's always a reason she can't. Or we'll make plans, and she'll change them last minute because something better came up." Heather's voice caught. "Last week, on my birthday, we were all at lunch, and she spent the whole time focused on this guy from our friend group, barely acknowledging me. When I left, she didn't even say goodbye. She promised to come over later to celebrate, but never showed."

"And what did you feel in that moment?"

"Frustrated. Angry." Heather's shoulders hunched. "But then I felt guilty for feeling that way. She's going through a lot right now with her divorce. I should be more understanding."

I leaned forward. "Heather, I noticed something interesting. When you tell me how you feel, you immediately shift to talking about her circumstances. You're living in her story instead of your own. What happens if we stay with your experience?"

Heather stared at the tissue in her hands. "I feel…disregarded." The word seemed to surprise her. "Like I'm not important enough to show up for."

"And what does that say to you about you?"

Her eyes teared up. "That I'm less than. That I don't matter."

"Ah," I said softly. "Now we're getting somewhere. Tell me, when Christina asks you to watch her kids, why do you say yes?"

"Because I want to help. Because I care about her." Heather paused, then added quietly, "Because it makes me feel valuable and like I deserve her friendship."

"Yes," I said. "You're trying to earn what should be freely given in friendship—regard and love for who you are, not what you do. You're still living by those old rules from childhood, where you let your worth depend on what other people need from you."

We sat with that for a moment.

Then Heather straightened her shoulders. "So what do I do? Cut her out of my life?"

"Let me ask you something different," I said. "What if this isn't about Christina? What if this is about you learning that you don't have to earn your worth? That you get to decide how people treat you?"

She nodded slowly. "I know I need to set stronger boundaries. I need to not hold this friendship so close anymore. But don't I owe her an explanation? A conversation about all this?"

"What would that conversation be for? For you to convince her to change, or for you to understand her behavior better?"

Heather was quiet for a long time. "Me, for me to try to convince her to be what I need," she finally admitted. "I don't want to hurt her, but I want her to understand how she hurt me. I want… I want her to know so she can fix it."

"And what if she can't? Or won't?"

"Then I guess I have to decide what I'm willing to accept." Heather looked up at me, something new flickering in her eyes. "Every time I've been around her lately, I can feel my inner light dimming. And I've just been stumbling around in the dark, hoping the light would turn back on."

I smiled. "The good news is, you know where the switch is now."

Sometimes, the hardest part of any relationship isn't recognizing when someone else has dimmed your light; it's acknowledging that you've been letting them. That's not about blame. It's about recognizing that while we can't control how others treat us, we absolutely can control what we accept.

"I don't want to hurt their feelings." I hear this all the time in my office. People staying in situations that drain them, accepting behavior that damages them, avoiding conversations that could heal them—all because they don't want to "hurt feelings." But often, we aren't really protecting other people's feelings. We're protecting ourselves from having to face our own.

When we say "I don't want to hurt them," what we're really saying is "I don't want to be the kind of person who causes pain." We've experienced hurt, felt its sharp edges, and we're so determined not to inflict that on others that we'll accept almost any discomfort to avoid it. We'll pour endlessly into one-sided friendships, tiptoe around necessary conversations, and exhaust ourselves trying to manage other people's emotions, all while our own needs go unmet.

But here's a truth that's harder to face: When we operate this way, we're not actually being kind—we're being avoidant. We're choosing the familiar pain of being disregarded over the uncertain pain of standing in the truth about our own experience. In doing so, we enable the very behaviors that are hurting us, creating a cycle where everyone loses: They never have to face the impact of their actions, and we never have to face our fear of being honest about our needs.

In all of this, we continue losing who we are.

THE INTERNAL COMPASS

Finding your way back to you starts with a simple but challenging shift: locating yourself in your own experience. Not what they did, but what you felt. Not what they should do differently, but what you need. Not how they need to change, but how you've lost yourself trying to change them.

We have become hardwired in believing our value comes from what we do, what we offer. We're taught to look outside ourselves for validation, to measure our worth by how well we meet others' expectations. Then we wonder why we feel lost, why every relationship feels like a negotiation, why we're constantly trying to earn what we already deserve.

This isn't easy work. It means finding yourself in stories you've been telling for years. It means discovering that maybe, just maybe, you've been focusing so hard on changing everyone and everything that you've forgotten who you are. We get so caught up in trying to fix everything around us that we don't realize we're the ones who need to be found.

How many times have you known something wasn't right but talked yourself out of that feeling because someone else seemed so certain? How often have you ignored your inner voice because someone else's was louder? We spend so much time trying to navigate by everyone else's stars that we forget we have our own internal compass.

Coming back to yourself is going to feel awkward at first. You're going to say how you really feel and the words won't come out right. You're going to set a boundary and feel guilty about it. You're going to try showing up authentically and part of you will want to crawl under a rock. This is normal. When you've spent years adapting to everyone else, being yourself feels like wearing shoes on the wrong feet.

The beauty in this work isn't in doing it perfectly. It's in the willingness to keep showing up, to keep listening to that internal compass even when the direction it points feels uncomfortable. When people finally start trusting their own experience, when they stop trying to earn what they already deserve, when they learn to value themselves first—everything changes. Not because others suddenly treat them differently, but because they finally know how to treat themselves.

So yes, it's going to be awkward. You'll have moments when you think it would've been easier just to focus on everyone else. Some of our ingrained habits can be tough to overcome! But the awkwardness is worth it. Because on the other side of that awkwardness is confidence in the real you: your real feelings, your real needs, your real power. That's what it means to live your own life instead of the one everyone else needs or even wants you to live. This isn't just good for you; it is good for everyone else.

FINDING YOUR STARTING LINE

BEN AND JACKIE had a volatile relationship, the kind where every session felt like walking through a minefield. The husband was sharp, charismatic, and used to being the loudest in the room. His wife was soft-spoken, demure, the type who'd say "It's my fault" while adding "and I hate you for it" under her breath.

One day, Jackie sat across from me, ready to put the nail in the coffin on the whole relationship after an event they attended. When I asked her to tell me about her experience—not about him, not about what he did, just about her—she started with, "When he did…"

I had to stop her and redirect her. "That's about him. Where are you in this?"

She tried again and found herself right back at his behavior. She paused.

I pressed her again. "Where are you in this?"

We did this five times, her frustration mounting.

After pressing her for the sixth time to focus on her, something clicked, and she said helplessly, "I don't know how to find me in this anymore."

That's your starting line.

Not where you want to be. Not where you think you should be. But where you actually are right now—no matter how far you have gotten from your internal compass.

EXTERNAL FOCUS

Jackie didn't want to admit that she had lost herself so deeply that she couldn't even articulate how she felt. But the fact that she recognized it gave us a starting point so we could do the work needed.

The question I end up asking most often in my office is: "Where are you in this?" Not where is your spouse in this. Not where are your kids in this. Not where is your boss in this. Where are YOU?

It's amazing how often we can talk about a situation that's bothering us without ever mentioning our own experience of it. We'll tell you what everyone else did wrong, what everyone else should have done differently, what everyone else needs to change. We can even tell you what everyone else is thinking and what their motive is. But ask us how we felt, what we needed, what we wanted? Suddenly, we're stumped.

I see it every week. The mother who can tell you everything her teenager is doing wrong and why but can't tell you what she's afraid of. The husband who can list every way his wife has disappointed him and her obvious motive in every case but can't articulate what he needs. The employee who can detail every mistake their boss has made and the reason for it but can't express their own desires for their career.

Why do we do this? Because it's safer looking out there than looking in here— within us. It's easier to focus on other people's stuff than to look at our own. It's more comfortable to be right than to be vulnerable.

Holding on to an external focus results in three behaviors that make life difficult for us: mind reading, control illusion, and pattern loop.

When we focus on everyone else, we give away our power. We put our happiness, our peace, our well-being in someone else's hands. And let me tell you something: Other people's hands are full. They have their own stuff to carry.

MIND READING

Your partner forgets something you told them, and you conclude that they don't care about you. A friend laughs at something you do, and you are convinced that they think you are weird or socially awkward. Another friend does not return your text, and you immediately believe they are mad at you. Your partner has a blank look on their face, and you believe they are disinterested in what you are saying; this leaves you thinking you are somehow bad.

When any event happens in our lives, we make a hypothesis about it. We want to make sense of the world. This is natural. That hypothesis is not the problem.

The problem happens when we take the sense we made of the situation (our hypothesis) as fact without collecting more information. We need more information from outside of ourselves but especially from inside of ourselves.

We may be carrying around past hurts. When those feelings get stirred up by a current event, we can make the mistake of seeing the current event just like the past event. Whatever motive and message came with that past event then seems certain to be present in the current event. Without knowing it, we have moved from hypothesis to certainty.

Fred, a software architect, came to see me because many of his relationships were not going the way he had hoped. He and his partner had constant arguments. He would leave them mumbling things under his breath about her. She would ask him, "What did you say?"

He'd reply, "Oh, it doesn't matter." However, what he was thinking was, You always say things like this, or Of course you think I am an idiot.

His partner did not think this at all. She was just frustrated with his behavior.

Fred and I were talking, and he exclaimed, "I know what you think of this!"

I had heard this phrase a few times in previous meetings. Frustrated, I said, "Fred, why are you thinking for me? Can I please participate in these conversations?"

He, being unaware of how often he mind reads people, said, "What do you even mean? You are part of these conversations!"

I responded, "Not when you tell me what I think. I am left out of the conversation. I am not being given the space to offer my thoughts. I am being told that you know exactly what I think. And I wonder if you'd be interested to know what I really think."

"Yes! I really do want to know!" he responded.

I went on to tell him my thoughts. He was amazed that he did not know what I was going to say. He then realized that this is an entrenched pattern for him. He grew up in a family where asking clarifying questions was not allowed.

As we worked together, he learned through our relationship that he could ask clarifying questions. He was able to do this with his partner and other trusted people in his life.

Fred isn't alone in this mind reading concept. Many of us do this. We assume we know what others are thinking, and we don't take the time to ask if we are right.

CONTROL ILLUSION

Mike, who was driven and accomplished in his career, had just been diagnosed with cancer. Not the "We caught it early, no big deal" kind, but the "We need to operate now, and even then we're not sure" kind. When I saw him after the surgery, he told me that people wanted to throw him a party to celebrate being "in remission."

There was just one problem—he wasn't in remission. That meant more treatment, more uncertainty, more of his life spinning out of his control.

Everyone wanted him to be happy, to be grateful, to be celebrating. But that wasn't true for him.

"I don't know how to tell people what I think about all this," he admitted during one session. "I don't know what I feel about it."

I stopped him. "Say that again."

"Well…I don't know how to tell people what I think about all this when they ask."

"How would you know what to tell them?" I asked.

"Yeah, I don't, because I don't know what I feel about it."

"So why do you think you could explain it to somebody else if you haven't even stopped long enough to consider how you feel?"

That was Mike's starting point, which is where many of us start: trying to figure out how to show up for others when we haven't even shown up for ourselves. Trying to meet expectations about how we should feel, what we should say, who we should be, when we haven't even discovered how we actually feel, what we actually want to say, who we actually are.

That's harder than you might think in a society like ours that rewards having all the answers. But showing up often means making things uncomfortable—for a purpose—and that may mean showing up without an answer. Mike's starting line meant having the courage to say, "I don't know how to feel about this yet. I don't know what to tell people."

Keep in mind that Mike is a guy who spent his entire career being The One Who Knows. When you're at this level of your career, that's literally your job—to be the one with answers, to be the one who can fix things, to be the one in control.

Then cancer comes along.

Suddenly, the guy who's used to giving orders is sitting in a hospital gown, waiting for someone else to tell him what's going to happen next. The guy who's used to having all the answers is faced with questions no one can answer for certain. The guy who's used to being in control…isn't.

"I've always been in control," he told me during one session, his voice tight with frustration.

"In your mind you have," I replied carefully, "but this diagnosis shows you you're not in control."

"Yeah," he said, looking away. "I don't really want to talk about that."

"I bet you don't," I said softly, "because now the premise of being out of control means that you might die."

He sat back, silent. See, that's the thing about control. It's not just about managing our daily lives; it's about managing our terror. Our terror of uncertainty, our terror of vulnerability, our terror of the fact that at the end of the day, we're all just walking around on a rock hurtling through space, pretending we know what's going to happen next.

Most of us aren't dealing with cancer diagnoses, but we're all dealing with our own version of this control illusion. Maybe it's the mom who thinks if she can just be involved enough, her kids will never get hurt. Maybe it's the husband who thinks if he can just make enough money, his wife will never leave. Maybe it's the friend who thinks if she can just say the right things, everyone will always like her.

This isn't about placing blame or saying relationships don't matter. Of course they matter. But when we make everything about the other person—their behaviors, their choices, their issues—we lose ourselves in the process. We hand over the keys to our emotional life and then wonder why we feel powerless.

What I've learned after a lifetime of watching people wrestle with control is that the things we try hardest to control are usually the things we're most afraid of losing. And the more we try to control them, the less we experience them.

Take another family I work with: They're so scared of conflict that they try to control every interaction. The mom measures her words so carefully that she barely speaks. The teenager is so afraid of her mom's reaction that she walks on eggshells. They're both so busy trying to control the situation that neither of them is actually in the relationship.

"I just want things to be perfect," the mom told me once.

"How's that working out for you?" I asked.

She laughed, but it wasn't a happy laugh. "It's exhausting."

"What if," I suggested, "instead of trying to make things perfect, you try to make them real? You give yourself permission to be you, and you give your daughter permission to be her?"

She looked at me like I'd suggested she try flying to the moon. "I don't know how to do that."

"None of us do, at first," I told her. "That's why we're here."

Want to know the truth that changed everything for Mike, the truth that changed everything for this family, the truth that could change everything for you?

The only real control you have is over yourself. Not over circumstances. Not over other people. Not over outcomes. Just you.

I know it sounds terrifying. It sounds like giving up. But here's the secret: When you give up the illusion of control, you gain the reality of influence. Influence comes when you know yourself so well that you can:

- Express your perspective without requiring others to validate it.
- Name your needs without demanding others meet them.
- Hold your boundaries without trying to control others' reactions.
- Stay present with uncertainty without trying to eliminate it.
- Explore others' experiences with curiosity instead of judging or trying to control them.

Mike learned this the hard way. He couldn't control his cancer, but he could control how he showed up to treatment. He couldn't control others' expectations of his recovery, but he could be honest about his own experience. He couldn't control the uncertainty, but he could stay present with it.

The question isn't "How can I control this situation?" The question is "How can I show up as myself in this moment?"

That's the real work: knowing yourself and choosing how you show up in the moment, not controlling outcomes. Because at the end of the day, the only person you have any real control over is yourself, and even that gets complicated when you've spent years giving your power away.

But that's okay. That's why we're here. That's where we start.

Before we can talk about where you're going, we need to get honest about where you are. Here are some questions to consider:

- When someone asks how you feel about something, do you automatically start talking about other people's behaviors instead?
- Do you find yourself constantly managing other people's emotions rather than processing your own?

- When making decisions, do you check what you want, or do you jump straight to what others might think?
- Can you name your core values without referencing other people's expectations?
- Do you know where your boundaries are, or do you only notice them after they've been crossed?

There's no judgment in these questions. They're just coordinates to help you locate yourself on the map. And if you're struggling to answer them—like Jackie, who couldn't find herself in her own story—that's valuable information too. Sometimes, knowing we're lost is the first step to finding our way.

PATTERN LOOP

Want to know something funny about patterns? We can spot everyone else's a mile away, but we're the last ones to see our own. We'll sit in my office and brilliantly analyze how a friend keeps choosing the wrong relationships, how a sibling keeps making the same career mistakes, how a coworker keeps undermining themselves. But turn that lens around? Suddenly, we're as blind as a bat in daylight.

But even when we can see our own pattern loop, it is not easy to stop.

Patterns don't just go away because we recognize them. Pattern loops are like those well-worn paths in your backyard. You can plant new grass, but the first time it rains, you and everyone else are still going to walk the same old route. The path is familiar. It's comfortable. It feels right, even when we know it's not serving us anymore.

The woman who keeps dating emotionally unavailable men because that's what feels "normal" after growing up with a distant father. The man who explodes in anger with his passive wife every time he feels scared because that's what his dad did with his mom. The teenager who is popular and achieves perfect grades yet continues to have judgmental friends and date critical girls because nothing is ever good enough at home and he feels like a failure underneath it all.

These patterns are survival strategies that worked at some point in our lives. Maybe they protected us. Maybe they got us the attention we desperately needed. Maybe they helped us cope with something that felt impossible to face.

The difference is, now we can stop and see ourselves in the picture. We can see the part we play in continuing our pattern loop. We can then see how our pattern begins to appear and we can respond differently.

Instead of letting that voice drive me into proving my worth by giving away the farm to keep people, I could pause and ask: "Where am I in this? What's actually true about my value versus what that old story is telling me?" That awareness doesn't make the voice disappear, but it does change how much power it has over my choices.

Using old patterns to navigate new situations is like wearing your childhood winter coat: At some point, you've got to admit it doesn't fit anymore.

Think about a recurring situation in your life, one that seems to keep showing up in different forms. Maybe it's relationships that follow the same path, maybe it's conflicts that feel eerily familiar, maybe it's emotions that keep catching you off guard. Now ask yourself:

- What's the pattern?
- When did you first notice it?
- What was happening in your life when this pattern developed?
- How has this pattern protected you?
- How might this pattern be limiting you now?

Looking at patterns in your life is one more way to find your starting point.

WHERE ARE YOU?

Take a moment right now and answer this question: Where are you? Not where you should be. Not where others want you to be. Not where you're trying to go. Where are you right now in your relationship with yourself?

Think about a recent interaction that left you feeling off-center. Could be with a partner, a parent, a friend, a coworker. Now answer these questions:

- What was your first instinct in responding?
- Where was your focus—on their behavior or your experience?
- Where were you in this situation?
- Were you having any mind reads?
- What were you trying to control at that moment?
- What old pattern were you playing out?

If your first instinct is to talk about other people's behaviors, that's your starting line. If you feel resistance to the questions themselves, that's your starting line. If you realize you don't know how to answer, that's your starting line. If you find yourself wanting to skip ahead to solutions, that's your starting line.

Most people start from one of four places:

The External Focus: You're so focused on others' behaviors, choices, and responses that you've lost the ability to locate yourself. Your feelings are reactions. Your choices are adaptations. Your life is about managing other people rather than knowing yourself.

The Mind Reading Trap: You make quick, certain conclusions about others' motives and hidden messages toward you when they interact with you. You do not hold these as hypotheses but as facts.

The Control Illusion: You're like Mike, the executive who had to face cancer. You've built your life around being the one with the answers, the one in control. Then something happens that shows you just how little control you actually have, and you don't know who you are without that illusion.

The Pattern Loop: You're stuck in patterns of interaction that aren't working, but you can't seem to find another way. You know something needs to change, but you keep repeating the same pattern.

Whatever your answer is, that's your starting line.

I've watched countless people stand at their starting lines. The people-pleaser learning to check their own needs first. The control-seeker learning to live with uncertainty. The conflict-avoider learning to stay present with discomfort. The externally focused learning to come home to themselves.

Your starting line is not your destiny. It's where you begin. And beginning, as messy and uncomfortable as it might be, is always better than staying stuck. The goal isn't to have the perfect starting point—there is no perfect starting point. The goal is to be honest about where you're starting from, to show up exactly as you are, even when it feels awkward.

You can't change what you won't acknowledge. You can't heal what you won't look at. And you can't discover your authentic self while pretending to be who you think everyone needs you to be.

Take a deep breath. Find your feet. This is your starting line.

In the chapters ahead, we're going to learn how to move forward from exactly where you are—not where you think you should be, not where others expect you to be, but where you actually are right now. Because that's where real change begins.

CHAPTER 3

STARTING WITH WHAT'S ACTUALLY THERE

"**I**'M FINE," MELISSA said, her smile tight, voice clipped. "Totally fine. Just tired."

Melissa had come to see me a month after being passed over for a major promotion—one she'd spent three years working toward, one she'd been repeatedly assured was hers to lose. Her boss had called it a "strategic redirection" when he gave the position to an outside hire with half her experience.

In the four weeks since, she'd maintained a flawless façade at work. She'd congratulated her new boss, offered to help with his transition, and kept every project moving forward without missing a beat. She'd been, by all external measures, the consummate professional.

But now, sitting in my office, the cracks were beginning to show.

"Tired, how?" I asked.

"Just regular tired. You know, work stuff." She waved her hand dismissively. "Anyway, I didn't come here to talk about being tired. I wanted some strategies for making sure this doesn't happen again. I need to understand what I did wrong so I can fix it."

"Before we go there," I said, "I'm curious about what's actually happening for you right now. Not what you're telling yourself should be happening, or what you're showing to others—but what's genuinely present in your experience."

She looked at me like I'd suggested we conduct the session underwater.

"What do you mean? I told you, I'm fine. I just want to get back on track."

"I hear that," I said. "And we'll definitely get to strategies. But first, I'm wondering if you'd be willing to try something. Could we just take a moment to check in with what's actually here right now? Without judging it or trying to change it—just noticing?"

She hesitated, then gave a small nod.

"Okay. Let's start with your body. If you're comfortable closing your eyes, great. If not, just soften your gaze and bring your attention inward. What physical sensations do you notice?"

She closed her eyes, and I watched as her carefully composed expression began to shift.

"My jaw is…really tight," she said after a moment. "And my shoulders are up by my ears, apparently." She let out a small, surprised laugh as she noticed the tension she'd been carrying.

"What else?"

"My chest feels…heavy. Like there's pressure on it. And my stomach is in knots."

"Just notice those sensations, without trying to change them," I guided. "Now, what about emotions? What feelings are present?"

The mask cracked further. Her eyes still closed, her face contorted briefly before she forced it back to neutrality.

"I'm angry." The words came out in a whisper. "I'm so angry I can barely breathe sometimes."

"Angry," I repeated, not as a judgment but as an acknowledgment. "What else?"

"Humiliated." Her voice caught. "I feel humiliated. Everyone knew how much I wanted that job, how hard I worked for it. And now every time I walk into a meeting, I feel like they're all thinking about how I wasn't good enough."

By now, tears were streaming down her face, the first she'd allowed herself since the promotion announcement.

"And I'm scared," she continued, the words coming faster now. "I'm scared that maybe they're right. Maybe I'm not good enough. Maybe I never will be."

When she finally opened her eyes, they were filled with a mixture of embarrassment and relief.

"Well, that was fun," she said, with a weak attempt at humor. "Sorry for the meltdown."

"No need to apologize," I said. "What just happened is incredibly important. You just made contact with what's actually there—the real emotions and sensations you've been carrying, rather than the 'fine' you've been presenting to the world."

This moment with Melissa captures one of the most fundamental principles of self-awareness: Before you can work with your experience, you have to acknowledge what's actually there. Not what you think should be there, not what others expect to be there, but what's genuinely present in your experience right now.

THE GAP BETWEEN REALITY AND "SHOULD"

Many of us have a complicated relationship with our experience. We're quick to judge it, reject it, try to fix it, or replace it with what we think we should be experiencing instead.

Melissa "should" have been fine. She was a professional. She prided herself on resilience. Getting emotional about work setbacks wasn't part of her self-image. By any rational measure, she should have moved on by now.

But "fine" wasn't what she was feeling. And her attempt to force "fine"—to overlay this "should" feeling on top of her actual experience—was creating a disconnect that made an already difficult situation even harder.

This gap between what we're actually experiencing and what we think we should be experiencing is the source of tremendous suffering. It's like trying to build a house on a foundation of clouds.

When I work with clients, the first thing I often ask them to do is to set aside the "should" and simply notice what's truly present in their experience. Not to judge it, not to fix it, not to transform it—just to acknowledge it.

For Melissa, this meant allowing herself to feel the anger, humiliation, and fear she'd been denying, instead of forcing the "professional" narrative that everyone expected from her. That honest recognition of her actual emotions was the first step toward authentic connection with herself and, ultimately, with others.

We live in a culture obsessed with emotional correctness. There are feelings we're supposed to have in certain situations and feelings we're not supposed to have.

When faced with a career setback, you're supposed to feel resilient and determined. When a colleague succeeds, you're supposed to feel happy for them. When given feedback, you're supposed to feel grateful. When working in a professional environment, you're supposed to keep emotions out of it.

But this emotional correctness extends far beyond our professional lives. It infiltrates every corner of our existence.

When someone gives you a gift, you're supposed to feel grateful, even if it's something you don't want or need. When you become a parent, you're supposed to feel instant, overwhelming love, not ambivalence, fear, or regret. When a relative dies, you're supposed to feel sad, not relieved, angry, or indifferent.

When you get married, you're supposed to feel it's the happiest day of your life, not anxious, uncertain, or overwhelmed. When your kid succeeds at something, you're supposed to feel proud, not jealous that you never had the same opportunities. When your friend shares good news, you're supposed to feel happy for them, not envious or threatened.

When your spouse wants sex, you're supposed to want it too, or at least feel bad that you don't. When you achieve a goal, you're supposed to feel satisfied, not empty or already focused on the next thing. When someone helps you, you're supposed to feel appreciative, not resentful of needing help in the first place.

When you make a mistake, you're supposed to feel appropriately remorseful, not defensive, shameful, or indifferent.

These emotional "shoulds" are so deeply ingrained that we often don't even question them. We just assume that if we're not feeling what we're "supposed" to feel, there's something wrong with us. We're broken, defective, or morally lacking in some fundamental way.

What's worse, we try to force ourselves to feel the "right" emotions, creating an exhausting internal struggle on top of whatever we're already dealing with. It's like trying to convince yourself to like cilantro when it tastes like soap to you; you might be able to pretend, but you can't change the actual experience.

This emotional correctness was even more pronounced for Melissa because of her professional identity. As a rising executive, she'd internalized messages about strength, resilience, and never letting them see you sweat. She prided herself on being rational, not emotional.

But now, facing a significant professional disappointment, she couldn't access the emotions she thought she should have. That disconnect was isolating her from herself and from potential sources of support.

"I haven't really talked to anyone about it," she admitted. "My friends ask how I'm doing, and I just say I'm fine and change the subject. I don't even know how to have the conversation. It feels pathetic to still be upset about this."

This gap between our authentic experience and the role we think we need to play is exhausting. It takes tremendous energy to maintain a false front, energy that could be directed toward genuine healing and growth if we were able to start with what's actually there.

THE FREEDOM IN "I DON'T KNOW"

Melissa began to practice something that felt both terrifyingly vulnerable and surprisingly liberating: She began to acknowledge the true state of her inner landscape, without judgment or immediate attempts to change it.

Sometimes, this meant acknowledging anger, hurt, or fear. Sometimes, it meant recognizing that she felt lost or confused about her next steps. Sometimes, it meant admitting, both to herself and eventually to trusted others, that she was struggling with self-doubt in a way she never had before.

These acknowledgments didn't immediately transform her experience. What they did do was create space for authentic connection, with herself and with others.

A pivotal moment came when Melissa finally had an honest conversation with a mentor she respected. Instead of giving her usual "I'm fine, just focusing on next steps" response when asked how she was doing, she said, "Actually, I'm really struggling with this. I'm dealing with a lot of anger and self-doubt, and I'm not sure what to do with those feelings in a professional context."

She'd been terrified to have this conversation, afraid that showing vulnerability would further damage her professional standing. But her mentor's response surprised her.

"Thank you for telling me," he said. "I've been through something similar, and it knocked me sideways for months. I questioned everything about my career path. No one really talks about how personally devastating these setbacks can be."

This willingness to start with what was actually there rather than what she thought should be there created the conditions for genuine connection rather than the false strength of denial and pretense.

Regardless of her mentor's response, she noticed a shift in herself. She felt 'lighter" and more curious about herself, others, and life.

Melissa discovered through this practice that accepting what's actually there doesn't mean you're stuck with it forever. In fact, acceptance is often the first step toward authentic change.

When we deny or reject our actual experience, we freeze it in place. We can't work with what we won't acknowledge. But when we accept our experience, when we create space to see it clearly without immediate judgment or attempts to change it, we create the conditions for organic transformation.

Three months into our work together, Melissa had an unexpected opportunity. A former colleague reached out about a position at a different company, one that would be a lateral move in terms of title, but with more creative latitude than her current role.

"Five years ago, I wouldn't have even considered it," she told me. "It wasn't the upward trajectory I'd mapped out. But now I'm actually excited about it. I realized that what I loved about the role I missed out on wasn't the title; it was the chance to build something new, to have more creative control over projects."

"And how are you feeling about your current job?" I asked.

She paused, checking in with herself rather than automatically responding with the expected answer.

"Still complicated," she said finally. "There's still some anger and disappointment there. But it's not consuming me the way it was. And there's also a strange sense of gratitude emerging—not for being passed over, which still sucked—but for the way it forced me to really look at what I want, not just what I thought I should want."

This was a huge shift from our early sessions, where Melissa had tried to force herself to feel what she thought she should feel. Now she was able to acknowledge her actual experience—complex, contradictory, and not always matching the expected narrative—without immediately judging it or trying to change it.

From that place of acceptance, clarity was beginning to emerge. Not the forced "I'm fine, moving on" of her initial response, but an authentic recognition of what truly mattered to her professionally.

"The weird thing is," she told me, "the more I let myself feel everything, including the anger and the self-doubt and the confusion, the more I also started to feel genuine curiosity about what might be next. Not because I should 'think positive' or 'look on the bright side,' but because the curiosity was actually there too, mixed in with everything else."

This is the nature of starting with what's actually there. It's not a destination you reach once and for all, but an ongoing practice of curiosity, honesty, and presence. A practice that, over time, creates the foundation for a more authentic relationship with yourself and with others.

The next time you find yourself thinking I should feel X or I shouldn't feel Y, try this simple practice:

1. Pause and take a breath.
2. Notice the "should" thought without judging yourself for having it.
3. Gently ask yourself, "What's actually here right now?"
4. Listen for the answer without trying to change it.

5. Acknowledge whatever you discover, whether it makes sense or not.

This simple practice can transform your relationship with yourself and with others. It won't make you perfect or ensure you always have the "right" feelings, but it'll bring you into contact with your experience as it is, creating the conditions for genuine awareness, growth, and connection.

WHY WE DON'T NATURALLY ASK THE QUESTION

CHAPTER 4

LETTING GO OF MIND READING

ONE OF THE biggest hurdles in us showing up fully with each other is that we all have mastered the art of mind reading—and yet we're terrible at it. We think we know how other people are thinking and feeling, so we become reactive to what we assume instead of simply asking them: "Hey, what are you thinking right now? How are you feeling?" and "What thoughts led to that? Why do you think those feelings surfaced for you?"

During one session, a mother and son revealed a conflict about the appointment set to see me, which was scheduled right after the son was to get off work. His mom had suggested they reschedule, but somehow that turned into a whole thing. Jeff came in hot: "She was disgusted with me that I wouldn't reschedule this."

I stopped him. "How do you know she was disgusted with you?"

"Well, because of the look on her face. It was all contorted like it always is when I disagree with her," he shot back. "I'm not an idiot."

"I'm not calling you an idiot," I said. "But you can't assume things. Let's ask her— conveniently, she's right here."

35

I turned to his mom. "Were you disgusted with him when he wouldn't reschedule?"

"No," she said quietly. "I mean, I was disappointed."

"See?" Jeff jumped in. "I'm a disappointment."

"Whoa, Mr. Global," I stopped him. "You're a disappointment? Is that what she said?"

I looked at his mom. "Does that resonate with you?"

"No," she said. "It was disappointing. The situation was disappointing."

Then she added something that made Jeff learn more about his mom, and his mom learn more about herself: "Honestly, I was disgusted with what I did. I hate being late. I don't like being late to appointments. I felt bad that we were going to be late."

There it was: Jeff had seen disgust on her face and made it all about him. He was right about the disgust, but completely wrong about its target.

How often do we do this? We see a look, we read a text, we interpret a tone of voice, and suddenly we're absolutely certain we know what someone else is thinking or feeling. We're usually wrong, by the way. But more importantly, we're usually projecting our own stuff onto others without recognizing it.

It's like we're all walking around with these interpretation machines in our heads, taking little bits of data—a facial expression, a tone of voice, a delayed text response—and running them through our personal filters of insecurity and past hurt. Then we take those interpretations and treat them as facts.

"She's disgusted with me."

"He doesn't respect me."

"They don't care about me."

The truth? Most of the time, we don't know what others are thinking or intending. We think we know, but we don't. And that not knowing is uncomfortable. So uncomfortable that we'd rather make up a story—even a painful one—than sit with uncertainty. It's even more uncomfortable to admit that what they said or did bothered us, and to ask the other person what's at the heart of their expression or words.

The mind-reading cycle goes something like this:

1. We observe a behavior.
2. We experience a difficult emotion.
3. We assign meaning to their behavior to make sense of the situation in our minds.
4. We experience another emotion (usually negative—hurt, anger, fear).
5. We act based on that other emotion (withdraw or attack).

At no point in this cycle do we check if our mind reading is accurate. We don't ask "Are you upset with me?" or "Is something bothering you?" Instead, we treat our assumptions as facts and respond accordingly.

This creates chaos because we're reacting to imagined scenarios. We're fighting battles that may not even exist.

Here's what most of us do when we feel attacked: We either attack back or we shut down. Both responses close the door to understanding.

The antidote to mind reading is curiosity—about others, yes, but first about yourself. When you can identify these internal processes, you regain the ability to respond thoughtfully rather than blindly.

Take for instance, Josh and Kristen.

Kristen opened with, "I need you to fix him."

She was devastated because she believed that Josh didn't value her. He was angry because she wouldn't listen. Both were certain their feelings came from what the other person wasn't doing. Both had lost themselves in trying to change the other.

That's how most couples start in my office: convinced that if their partner would just change, everything would be fine. They don't realize that's not what my job is.

When something hurts us, when someone disappoints us, when life doesn't go as planned, our first instinct is to judge. We judge others for causing our pain. We judge ourselves for allowing it. We judge the situation for existing at all. Judgment feels powerful. It feels like protection.

But judgment keeps us stuck. It locks us into seeing things one way: my way, their way, the right way, the wrong way. And as long as we're judging, we can't see what's really happening.

Another couple sat in my office going through their usual dance. She was furious about his behavior. He was defensive about her reactions. Both were certain they knew exactly what the other person was doing wrong. I asked them to pause for a moment and get curious instead of certain.

"What if you're not seeing the whole picture?" I asked. "What if there's more to this story than either of you realizes?"

That's when things got interesting. Because once they got curious—really curious, not just waiting for their turn to speak—they began discovering things they'd never seen before. He wasn't just being difficult; he was terrified of failing. She wasn't just being controlling; she was scared of being abandoned. Behind every judgment was a story neither of them had known to explore.

Curiosity opens doors that judgment keeps firmly shut. It lets us ask questions like: What's really going on here? What am I not seeing? What's beneath this reaction? What if there's more to this story?

Curiosity takes courage. It's safer to stay in judgment, to keep believing we know exactly what's happening and exactly whose fault it is. Curiosity asks us to admit we might not know. It means we might have to change how we see things. We might have to change how we see ourselves. And that's scary.

I had a client once who was convinced his wife was just lazy about their sex life. He believed that he had it all figured out: She was using it to manipulate him. She didn't care about his needs. She was probably having an affair.

When I asked him to get curious about what else might be happening, he resisted. Because as long as he was judging, he didn't have to feel the fear underneath his anger. He didn't have to face the possibility that maybe they'd both lost their way to each other, which was even more terrifying for him.

Let me share with you something I learned early in my career that made me want to quit being a therapist: According to one of the leading research groups in the field of marriage (the Gottman Institute), about 70% of the problems in your relationships do not have a resolution. Let that sink in. More than two-thirds of what you're fighting about? No resolution.

I thought about walking away from the profession. I thought, what's the point? If we can't resolve most of the problems, why even try? But through my work over the years, I have come to know the true power of conquering such a low statistic and flipping it on its head: These conflicts don't need to be solved; they need to be better understood.

When we seek to understand each other, conflicts dissipate, and we learn how to co-exist, while acknowledging that multiple things can be true at the same time. The Gottman Institute even showed this in their later research.

Let me show you what this looks like.

I had a couple—let's call them Frank and Martha—who had been fighting about the same issues for twenty years. He needed time to decompress after work. She needed connection. This wasn't going to change; it was part of their fundamental wiring.

On the surface, Frank and Martha were fighting about screen time—not their kids' screen time, but his. Every day when Frank got home from work, he'd spend about fifteen minutes on his phone. Martha saw this as him choosing technology over family time.

"You're always on your phone when you get home!" Martha accused. "You don't care about being present with us!"

Instead of defending or attacking, I got curious. "Frank, what's happening for you when you get home?"

He sighed, then said, "I race home because I want to be here. But I need just fifteen minutes to decompress. I could just walk into another room and tell them to go screw themselves, but I don't. I do try to be present. Yes, I'm on my phone, but I just need fifteen minutes to transition."

I looked at Martha. "What would it be like if he said to you, 'Hey, I need to decompress. I've had a long day. I need about fifteen minutes to think my own thoughts and not answer a lot of questions about my day, but I can't wait to be with you after I reset'?"

Her face softened. "That…that would be completely different."

"So go ahead and ask him what he needs," I encouraged her.

"What do you need in those first few minutes home?" she asked him.

"I just need fifteen minutes to decompress from my day. Fifteen minutes to zone out, think my thoughts. Engaging in a thoughtful conversation right away takes it out of me. I have been engaging with clients all day. It's not that my clients are more important than you. It will simply help me feel like I can be fully present with you and the kids afterward. So if I take the time to do that, what would help you feel more connected when I get home?" he asked her in return.

"Can I be close to you while you do that? Can I come sit with you and not say anything, but just be with you?"

The situation hadn't changed. Frank still needed his transition time, Martha still wanted connection. But curiosity opened a door that mind reading had kept firmly shut. Instead of trying to change each other, they got curious about how to work with who they actually were. For the first time, they were curious about each other's experiences instead of certain.

Curiosity doesn't require us to abandon our experience. It asks us to make room for even more understanding of our experience and of others'. To look beyond our first reaction and our instant judgment. To ask, with genuine interest: What else might be true here?

THE PRACTICE OF CURIOSITY

So how do we change this? How do we move from mind reading to curiosity?

1. Start With Yourself: Before you ask anyone else questions, get curious about your own experience. What are you feeling, thinking, experiencing and believing? What do you really need?
2. Ask Open Questions: Not "Why did you do that?" but "What was happening for you then?" Not "How could you?" but "Help me understand."
3. Listen for Understanding, Not Agreement: You don't have to agree with someone's perspective to be curious about it.
4. Stay in the Question: When you feel yourself wanting to defend or attack, that's your cue to get curious instead. (It helps to remind yourself that you are okay even when you are misunderstood or wrong.)

Frank and Martha still have different needs around transition time after work. But now, instead of fighting about it, they're curious about it.

Martha asks, "How was your day? Do you need some decompression time?"

Frank checks in. "I need about fifteen minutes. How are you doing? What do you need from me after that?"

They're dancing with their differences instead of trying to eliminate them.

Since this is a new practice for many of us, I want to equip you with some questions that you can practice with and use in situations that you may encounter.

QUESTIONS FOR SELF-EXPLORATION

1. When triggered/upset:
   - "What am I feeling in my body right now?"
   - "What does this remind me of from my past?"
   - "What am I afraid might happen?"
   - "What do I need in this moment?"
   - "Is this reaction about the current situation or something deeper?"
2. When making judgments:
   - "Why does this bother me so much?"
   - "What story am I telling myself about this?"
   - "What would it mean about me if I was wrong?"
   - "Am I reacting to protect myself from something?"
   - "What am I assuming without evidence?"

QUESTIONS FOR UNDERSTANDING OTHERS

1. When someone is expressing emotion:
   - "What's this like for you?"
   - "Can you help me understand what you're experiencing?"
   - "What do you need right now?"
   - "What's the hardest part about this for you?"
   - "How long have you been feeling this way?"
2. During conflict:
   - "What matters most to you about this?"

- "How did you see that situation?"
- "What were you hoping would happen?"
- "What feels important to protect here?"
- "What would make you feel more understood?"

3. For deeper connection:
- "What does that mean to you?"
- "How did you come to see things that way?"
- "What's shaped your perspective on this?"
- "What do you wish I understood about your experience?"
- "What feels unseen or unheard?"

Eric and Max were best friends who would always get together on Wednesday nights to check in with each other and hang out. Eric became frustrated because Max kept checking his phone and texting instead of being engaged in what Eric was telling him. Instead of asking why Max was being so rude (his mind read), Eric practiced getting curious. First, he asked himself what he was feeling and what he was needing. He determined that he was feeling dismissed and that he needed clarification.

He said, "Hey, man, I notice you're checking your phone a lot lately instead of listening to me. What's going on for you?"

Max paused, then shared that his mother had been having health issues. He was anxiously waiting for updates from his sister who lived closer to their mom. He hadn't told Eric yet because he didn't want to outwardly worry about something that might be nothing.

This opened up a whole new conversation. Eric's anger transformed into concern and connection. But first, he had to get curious instead of assuming he knew the story.

The key is moving from "I know why you did that" to "Help me understand." From "You always…" to "What's happening for you?" From judgment to curiosity.

These questions aren't a script; they're doorways to deeper understanding. The specific words matter less than the genuine desire to understand rather than prove a point or defend a position.

Think about a conflict in your life. Is there a time that you can see, in hindsight, you were mind reading instead of investigating what was happening? What would have happened if you got curious instead of defensive? What might you have learned if you started asking questions instead of making assumptions?

Curiosity isn't about getting it perfect. It's about staying open to understanding, even when (especially when) you think you already know the answer. It's about learning to ask better questions. Questions that open us up instead of shut us down. Questions that lead us deeper into understanding of ourselves first and others second.

CHAPTER 5

LETTING GO OF THE CONTROL ILLUSION

SATURDAY AFTERNOON TRAFFIC in Dallas is bad on a good day. This wasn't a good day.

I was driving to my son's baseball game on the east side of the city, an hour's drive from home in the best conditions. As I merged from an express lane, traffic ahead came to a sudden stop. Fortunately, I had a long runway to slow down in my truck. Until I didn't.

A sedan to my right abruptly cut in front of me, forcing me to slam on my brakes. My tires screeched against the asphalt as I barely avoided hitting him. Then, inexplicably, he continued to maneuver his car to block me each time I tried to change lanes to get away from him.

My hand found the horn, and I leaned on it. Not a quick "Hey, I'm here" honk. This was a full minute-and-a-half assault that had other drivers looking over in alarm.

My heart hammered in my chest. My vision tunneled. My knuckles whitened on the steering wheel. At that moment, I was ready to engage in battle. Which battle? I honestly couldn't tell you! I just knew I was totally keyed up!

Then a small voice in my head: Lee, come back to yourself. Come back to yourself.

I was so far outside myself I could barely hear it. My body was flooded with a white-hot intensity that had obliterated any sense of who I was and what I was doing.

What are you experiencing? I asked myself, trying to find my way back.

Fury! I'm feeling EXTREME fury.

What's behind that feeling?

Anger.

And what's behind that anger?

It took me a moment to find the answer, but when it came, it was clear as day: fear.

The fear hit me first. When he cut me off, I was genuinely afraid I was going to crash. My truck could have plowed into him. We both could have been seriously hurt. That fear instantly transformed into anger, which propelled me forward into a blinding fury.

I was trapped between a concrete barrier and this unpredictable driver, and I couldn't escape. The feeling of being cornered amplified everything.

As this realization washed over me, I noticed groups of young girls in cheer uniforms walking across an overpass. At the same time, my phone blared an emergency alert: "Active Shooter at the Convention Center." (Which turned out to be a false alarm.)

My fear spiked again, but differently. I felt an overwhelming urge to gather all those girls into my truck and get them to safety. My protective instincts roared to life, taking me back to when my own daughters were that age. I would have crushed anyone who threatened them.

In that moment of clarity, I recognized myself again. I wasn't just a man consumed by fury; I was a protector. That's who I am at my core. The fear had transformed into a desire to shield those who seemed vulnerable, which is far closer to my true nature than the fury I'd been feeling. I took a deep breath and thought, They're not mine to protect right now.

Taking those deep breaths, finding my center again, I felt the fury begin to subside. Still shaken, I was returning to myself. By the time I arrived at my son's game, I had regained enough composure to handle a frustratingly biased umpire without getting ejected.

Had I shown up still in the grip of that highway anger, the outcome could have been very different.

THE INTERNAL CHAOS

We all experience moments when emotions overtake us, when we're so far outside ourselves that we barely recognize our thoughts and behaviors. These are moments of internal chaos.

The chaos doesn't always look like fury. Sometimes, it's the frozen feeling when your boss criticizes your work in front of colleagues. Sometimes, it's the spiral of anxious thoughts at 3 AM that prevents you from sleeping. Sometimes, it's the numbness you feel when faced with a decision you don't want to make.

Whatever form it takes, internal chaos has one defining characteristic: It disconnects you from yourself. This disconnection creates a fundamental problem. You can't understand your relationships with others when you've lost your relationship with yourself.

At its core, this is the difference between intrapersonal understanding, knowing your own internal landscape, and interpersonal understanding, knowing how to bring that self-awareness into your interactions with others. Without the first, the second becomes impossible.

When you're disconnected from yourself, you can't:

- Identify what you're actually feeling.
- Understand why you're feeling it.

- Make decisions that align with your values.
- Connect authentically with others.
- Respond rather than react.

You become like a ship without a rudder, tossed about by emotional storms you neither understand nor control.

I've come to think of our emotions as dashboard lights in a car. They're not there to annoy you. They're there to give you information about what's happening under the hood.

Consider these emotional indicators:

Forward-Moving Emotions (like anger, frustration, or excitement) push us to act, to move, to do something.

Backward-Moving Emotions (like fear, shame, or sadness) pull us away from action, making us withdraw or freeze.

When we experience a forward-moving emotion (like anger), it's often covering a backward-moving emotion (like fear). My fury on the highway was the surface emotion, but fear was driving it all.

Similarly, someone who appears aloof or insensitive might be experiencing frustration, which often masks a deeper feeling of shame, of not being good enough or worthy of connection.

These emotional patterns are signaling something important about what's happening inside us.

If you've ever been in a car with someone who keeps adjusting the temperature every two minutes, you know what it's like to watch someone completely unaware of their internal state trying to fix it externally. They're hot, they're cold, they're hot again—but they never stop to ask themselves what's really going on inside.

We do this with our emotions all the time. We're constantly adjusting our external world, trying to fix feelings we haven't even identified yet. We focus on what others are doing wrong instead of understanding our own experience. We're like that person frantically adjusting the thermostat when what we really need is to check our own temperature.

Think about how often we jump to extremes in our relationships, either taking all the blame or none of it. The truth usually lives somewhere in between, but we can't find that middle ground until we're willing to look at ourselves honestly.

One of the clearest signals that we've lost touch with our inner world is when we become obsessed with controlling others, when we believe that if we can just make them change, everything will be better.

CONTROLLING OTHERS' BEHAVIORS

John was convinced he needed help forcing his parents to make "better" decisions. His mother's cancer had come back, and John was ready to move heaven and earth to get her to the best oncologist in the country. He'd researched treatments, contacted specialists, even offered to pay for everything himself. But his mother refused. She "didn't want to put him out."

John was furious. Here he was, trying to save his mother's life, and she wouldn't let him. He came to me wanting strategies to make his parents see reason. But what he really needed was to understand what was happening inside him.

"Where are you in this?" I asked him.

He looked at me like I'd grown a second head. "What do you mean? I'm trying to help my mother!"

"I hear that," I said. "But let's pause for a minute. Before we talk about making them do anything, tell me what this is bringing up for you."

It took some time, but finally, John got quiet. "I can't lose her," he said. "Not yet. Not like this."

Now we were getting somewhere. Once John could see that his pushing wasn't about not being allowed to find the best treatment for his mother but about the terror of losing her, something shifted. He was able to listen when his parents explained their perspective.

His mother hated flying. The thought of spending her remaining time in airports and strange cities filled her with dread. She and his father had made peace with her prognosis. They wanted to focus on enjoying their time together, not chasing miracle cures.

Was this what John wanted? No. But once he understood himself better, he could understand them better too. He could see that his need to fix everything was getting in the way of connecting with his parents during this precious time.

This is what happens when we're not aware of our own stuff. We push, we demand, we try to control, all while thinking we're just trying to help. We're so focused on making others see our perspective that we can't hear theirs. It's only when we understand our own fears, our own needs, our own grief, that we can make space for others to show up authentically in the interaction.

John didn't give up on wanting his mother to live. But he did give up trying to force his solution on her. Because he finally understood this wasn't about him being right or wrong; it was about him learning to respect his mother's choices even when they differed from his own.

My family was in the midst of a home renovation project. Workers were in and out of our home so frequently it resembled Interstate-35 on a Friday afternoon, complete with congestion, noise, and the occasional unexplained delay. Drywall dust had formed its own ecosystem in our house, coating everything like a thin layer of construction-scented snow.

After a particularly grueling day at the office (where, ironically, things were less chaotic than at home), I walked through our front door and immediately spotted it: a full-sized bathtub sitting in the entryway. On our hardwood floor. Our newly finished hardwood floor.

My brain almost short-circuited. *This is going to scratch the floor beyond repair!* I thought, my blood pressure climbing faster than the renovation costs. *Who in their right mind would do this?!*

I found my wife in the kitchen and began interrogating her like she was the prime suspect in a high-profile crime drama. My tone was somewhere between "disappointed parent" and "traffic officer who just caught you doing 90 in a school zone." I could not hide my frustration.

Mid-questioning, I caught sight of her expression. That look on her face—part hurt, part "Are you seriously doing this right now?"—was like a bucket of cold water to my bathtub-scratched-floor-obsessed brain. I realized I was about to unleash a tirade on one of the most valuable humans in my life—over a bathtub. This runaway train of frustration needed emergency brakes applied immediately.

So how do we show up when everything in us wants to control others' actions? Here's what I've learned:

1. **Know Your Desired Outcome for You:** How do you desire to act? What do you desire to say? In this case, I wanted to calmly ask my wife why the bathtub was in the living room and what the plan was to move it from there without scratching the wood floors.

2. **Stay in Your Body:** Notice when you're moving toward the desire to lash out or shut down. That's your cue to take a deep breath, feel your feet on the ground, and remember who you are and where you are. Stay grounded.

3. **Speak Your Perspective, Not Your Anger:** I wanted to express my concern with the bathtub on the wood floor and ask to solve the problem together. I needed to clearly articulate the impact of what was going on and what needed to change.

4. **Be Willing to Be Vulnerable:** Change happens in the vulner-
    able moments. Growth happens in the vulnerable moments.
    Love happens in the vulnerable moments.

Thank God I am married to an amazing woman who is full of grace
for me. She allowed me the space to catch my breath and finish the
conversation in a different way.

As for the bathtub? We moved it without incident. No scratches,
no permanent damage to the floor or our relationship. Crisis averted.
We were able to create a different appliance staging area that did not
have the threat of damage.

Staying connected to yourself and out of the control illusion begins
with the most fundamental relationship we'll ever have: the one with
ourselves. It's about learning to trust the landscape of your inner world,
to believe that your thoughts, feelings, and experiences are valid.

As we've talked about, many of us spend years living as strangers to
ourselves. We learn to quiet our inner voice, to doubt our instincts, to
apologize for taking up space. We become expert translators of other
people's expectations, while losing the language of our own soul. But
true connection to yourself starts with a radical act of self-acceptance:
believing that you are enough.

What does it mean to trust yourself? It's more than confidence.
It's a deep, cellular knowing that your feelings are real, your experiences matter, and your intuition is a wisdom worth listening to. It's
understanding that your worth isn't determined by how perfectly you
perform or how well you manage others.

Trusting yourself means:

- honoring your emotions, even the uncomfortable ones
- recognizing that your first response is often your most honest one
- understanding that your boundaries are not walls, but acts of
  self-love

- accepting that you don't need to justify your feelings to anyone
- knowing that your sensitivity is a strength, not a weakness

Your feelings are not inconvenient. Your thoughts are not a burden. Your needs are not too much.

You are valuable.

From this place of true connection, true knowing of yourself, true self-trust, everything changes. Your relationships transform. Your boundaries become clear. Your choices become intentional. You stop apologizing for the space you occupy and start celebrating the unique terrain of your being. Showing up like that will have influence on others and on situations in a powerful way. It is way more powerful than the control illusion.

CONTROLLING OTHERS' VIEW OF US

Another manifestation of internal chaos appears when we place our value in how others see us. When we don't know who we are or don't believe in our inherent worth, we try to earn it through what we do for others. People pleasing is one of the biggest ways we try to control how others view us.

I had this beautiful couple in my office. They were both strikingly attractive people, the kind that turn heads when they walk into a room. But underneath that polished exterior, they were completely disconnected from themselves.

The wife would tell me about all the things her husband was doing wrong in her eyes. He was a people pleaser through and through, jumping up the moment anyone said they needed anything and providing them with it. She was annoyed by it, and he was perplexed because he thought he was doing the right thing. As per usual, I kept asking them both to stay with themselves, to look at their own experience rather than focusing on each other.

"I don't trust it," she finally said one day.

Aha! Now this was finally getting deeper than just being annoyed.

"What don't you trust?" I asked.

"If he's doing those things for everyone, how is it anything special when he does those same things for me? Also, I don't trust it with our kids," she said, getting us even closer.

"Tell me more about that," I said.

She leaned forward, her voice tightening with emotion. "Our kids are watching him give and give until there's nothing left. They're learning that's what relationships look like: having no boundaries, always saying yes, putting yourself last. I see them starting to do it too, feeling like they have to take care of everyone else's feelings before their own. How will they ever learn to know themselves if they're always focused on what everyone else needs?"

Now we were getting somewhere. This wasn't just about her frustration with her husband's behavior. She was seeing the long-term impact on their children's development, how they were learning to navigate relationships by watching their father's pattern of people pleasing. Would they grow up thinking love meant losing yourself in service to others? Would they know how to set healthy boundaries in their own relationships?

Her husband sat quietly for a moment, letting this sink in. "I just want them to be kind, giving people," he finally said.

"There's a difference between choosing to give and not knowing how to say no," I replied. "One comes from knowing who you are. The other comes from not knowing who you are at all."

When we place our value in other people's hands, we become puppets, dancing to everyone else's tune. We think we're being good people, think we're being caring and giving, but really? We're just trying to earn our right to exist.

Here's the truth: Your value isn't something to be proven. It isn't in what you do for others. It's not in how much they approve of you or how well you meet their expectations. Your value is inherent.

It's like I tell my clients: You don't have to earn the right to take up space in this world. You don't have to justify your existence through constant service to others.

When we finally understand this, we can still choose to serve others, still choose to be giving and kind. But we're doing so from a place of fullness rather than emptiness, from choice rather than compulsion.

This is where true generosity comes from—not from trying to earn our worth, but from already knowing it.

THE POWER OF STAYING CONNECTED TO YOURSELF

Learning to stay connected to your inner world even when external events are chaotic isn't just a nice idea. It's a practical skill that can transform your interactions with others.

A friend of mine, John, was telling me a story about an interaction he had with a suite mate in his building. John told me how this little guy with a big attitude who fancies himself a real piece of work decided to mock him in front of his coworkers. He was telling me about his instinct to react and to put him in his place (and trust me, John could have). John and I had been talking about how to stay inside yourself lately, so he was fired up telling me this story!

Instead, he said he thought to himself, Stay inside yourself. Stay connected to who you are. Do not value yourself based on what's about to happen.

When the suite mate made his little digs, John described himself as just looking at him and said, "Okay." Nothing more. In the awkwardness of him trying to poke at John and not getting any reaction whatsoever, his coworkers spoke up, defending John against his comments, while he shrank into himself. Why? Because John stayed in his own inner world instead of being pulled into this guy's world.

When you operate like this, people around you can feel it. They know which side is safer.

That's what internal awareness gives us: not a perfect life, not a problem-free existence, but a reliable way to check our own inner temperature and respond from a place of centeredness rather than reactivity.

Let me emphasize that understanding yourself is the foundation for understanding others. You have to understand your own emotional landscape before you can effectively navigate relationships with others.

This doesn't mean you become self-absorbed. Quite the opposite. When you understand yourself better, you're better equipped to truly see and understand others. You're less reactive, more responsive. You're not constantly projecting your unexamined stuff onto everyone else.

However, one of the hardest parts of developing self-awareness is learning to sit with uncomfortable emotions instead of immediately trying to fix them or blame them on someone else. It's like building a muscle—it gets stronger with practice, but the process isn't always pleasant.

Here's a simple practice to help you begin exploring your inner world:

Think about something that's bothering you about someone else right now. Maybe it's your partner leaving dishes in the sink, your coworker talking too loudly on the phone, or your friend always being late. Now, work through these questions:

1. What is the external behavior that bothers you?
2. What emotion does this behavior bring up in you? (Dig deeper than "annoyed" or "frustrated." Perhaps you feel disregarded, unsafe, or invisible.)
3. When else have you felt this emotion in your life?
4. What does this emotion tell you about what matters to you?
5. How would you like to behave in this given situation?

Notice how none of these questions focus on changing the other person's behavior. That's intentional. Self-awareness isn't about controlling others; it's about understanding ourselves.

The greatest barrier to self-understanding is the chaos that disconnects us from ourselves. When we can't identify what we're feeling or why we're feeling it, we lose our internal compass. We react rather than respond, often making situations worse in the process.

In the Christian tradition, the greatest commandment is to love God, and the second is to love your neighbor as yourself. Note the sequence: You must know and love yourself before you can truly love others. This isn't selfish—it's essential.

From a secular standpoint, the principle is the same. Without self-awareness, without understanding your own emotions and reactions, relationships become battlegrounds rather than connections.

Coming back to yourself isn't a one-time achievement. It's a skill that requires practice. Here are some ways to build that skill:

1. **Create Space for Awareness:** When emotions run high, pause if possible. Take three deep breaths. This gives your rational brain a chance to come back online.

2. **Get Curious, not Judgmental:** Don't beat yourself up for feeling what you feel. Ask what this emotion might be telling you. What do you need to ask for?

3. **Connect With Your Body:** Strong emotions always have physical components. Noticing these physical sensations can help ground you.

4. **Challenge Your Control Illusion:** Am I seeking control of others' actions? Of their view of me? What influence do I want to have by staying connected to who I am?

5. **Return to Your Values:** Ask what matters to you in this situation, beyond the immediate emotional reaction.

6. **Determine Your Desired Outcome:** How do I want to show up (or behave) in this situation?

The path back to yourself and out of the control illusion begins with recognizing when you've lost connection. The internal chaos that makes you feel out of control is your first clue that something important needs your attention.

Like my moment on the highway, these episodes of disconnection can be frightening. But they also present opportunities to deepen your understanding of yourself, to strengthen the muscles of self-awareness, to live more intentionally, and to discover the power of your influence.

The next time you feel overwhelmed by emotions or caught in a conflict that seems impossible to resolve, come back to yourself. The path through chaos always begins within.

LETTING GO OF THE PATTERN LOOP

RELATIONSHIP PATTERNS CAN repeat over and over even when they are unhealthy. We may be able to see this pattern loop and not know how to get out of it. Knowing what a healthy relationship pattern looks like can help.

Relationships are made up of three parts:

- view of self
- view of others
- view of interactions between self and others (style)

Both the style of the self and the style of the other interact to form a relationship pattern. This is like a dance or pendulum between two people. If the view of self and other is healthy and accurate, the style or expression of the person will be as well. But if the person does not know themselves or has false beliefs about themselves, they will have false beliefs about others and their style as well. This causes unnecessary conflict and pain in the dance they do with others.

Healthy patterns emerge when both parties know and value themselves accurately, express themselves without indictment of the other, and explore the other without judgment. The interactions between them accurately reflect who they really are, and the atmosphere for those interactions is safe and loving.

Unhealthy patterns emerge when one or both parties do not know or value themselves accurately, and express themselves with mind reading, indictment, judgment, and control. The interactions between them do not accurately reflect who they are, and the atmosphere for those interactions is unsafe and fearful.

Healthy patterns grow and are flexible. Unhealthy patterns stagnate and are rigid; they also tend to repeat even when they become unwanted. This is called the pattern loop.

Each person has a part to play in the pattern. The root of the health or unhealth of a pattern rests on the self, specifically on whether the person knows their value as a human being or not. This may seem like a simple concept, but it is actually difficult to believe and hold onto.

Our value as human beings is high and equal to that of others. Value is inherent in being human. It is not something that can be gained or lost through our actions or performance. We cannot add to it or decrease it.

Value is not the same as identity. Identity is made up of both our uniqueness (personality) and our commonness with others. We are genetically more than 99% the same and less than 1% different, but we are all 100% valuable.

So why is it difficult to believe and hold onto this basic truth? It is challenged everyday by our surroundings (and it has been since we were born). We hear things like "What value do you add to the company?" and "What is your net worth?" almost weekly. We identify people by what they do or by their diagnosis. He is a basketball player, or he is autistic. We blur the line between what we do and who we are.

We develop a core narrative about who we are that is simply inaccurate. This narrative starts early and continues to form all our lives.

The good news is that we can recognize it and begin to tell ourselves the truth and act accordingly.

Let me tell you about the start of my own core narrative. I was the baby of the family—and when I say baby, I mean my closest sibling was eleven years older than me. By the time I was learning to ride a bike, my oldest brother was heading off to an Ivy League school. While I was struggling with elementary school math, my sister was already running her own company. There was a twenty-five-year gap between the oldest and me, which meant I spent my childhood watching a highlight reel of success I couldn't possibly match.

My Achilles' heel became this gnawing belief that I wasn't enough. Not smart enough, not successful enough, not…well, just not enough. My parents had me tested because I was doing so poorly in school. I remember sitting in that psychologist's office, convinced I was about to be exposed as the family failure. When she stopped the testing early, I thought I'd performed so badly she couldn't even continue. Turns out, my IQ was not a problem—but that information bounced right off the armor of self-doubt I'd built.

You see, it wasn't about intelligence. It was about this story I'd written in my head: that I had to be exceptional just to be acceptable. That I couldn't just show up as myself. I had to show up as some perfect version of myself, or some version that met others' unspoken expectations of who I was supposed to be. That became my style of relating.

My core narrative caused me to form a relationship style where I believed I wasn't enough; I had to entertain others to make them want to spend time with me. My style attracted others whose style was to depend on me. This became exhausting, but I could not stop. I was in a pattern loop, and I didn't know how to change it. Thankfully, I learned how to deal with my core narrative, change my style, and stop the pattern loop I was caught in.

Even now though, decades later, with a successful practice and a wonderful family, that old style can reappear in my life. Instead of letting the voice of my core narrative drive me into proving my worth by giving away the farm to keep people, I can pause and ask: "Where am I in this? What's true about my value versus what that old narrative is telling me?"

That awareness doesn't make the voice disappear, but it does change how much power it has over my choices. I can choose to risk acting on my true value, and when I do, the old pattern does not emerge, a new one does, not with everyone, but with many people. (Patterns require two people to participate.)

A specific example of when my core narrative raised its ugly voice recently was when I was preparing to speak on a panel at a large event. As I sat waiting for my turn to speak, that familiar voice in my head started up: "You don't know enough about this. You're not that bright. You're not a clear communicator." The chaos of self-doubt threatened to disconnect me from my authentic self.

In that moment, I had to consciously recognize what was happening: "This is that old story." As one of my closest trusted friends said to me, "You are not there to convince people you are smart. You are there because you ARE smart."

I reminded myself: "Just show up. Be yourself." I stopped scripting my answers and spoke naturally. It wasn't perfect, but it was authentic. And I was okay with that.

I call these sorts of experiences "emotional scar tissue."

A few years ago, I experienced debilitating back pain that lasted nine months. I could barely walk, couldn't sit, and often had to work standing up, hunched over in agony. When I finally found the right doctor and had surgery, the relief was immediate.

During my recovery, I worked with a physical therapist who used techniques like dry needling to interrupt the pain pathways in my nervous system. She explained that even after an injury heals, our bodies remember that pain pathway. When pressure from the environment occurs, our nerves follow these established pathways and our body remembers it as pain again—even when there's no actual damage happening.

She went on to tell me that through this process of needling that is disrupting these pathways, we teach the body new patterns that don't automatically associate certain sensations with pain.

Our emotional responses work the same way, hence the emotional scar tissue. Even after we've processed difficult experiences and grown from them, the neural pathways remain. If we encounter situations that trigger similar feelings, we can find ourselves responding with old styles before we even realize what's happening.

This doesn't mean we haven't healed; it means healing is an ongoing process that requires continued awareness. We may never completely erase the neural pathways created by painful experiences, but we can become aware when we're following them. With awareness comes choice, and with choice comes freedom.

CORE NARRATIVES AND MIND READING

"She's going to leave me," Alex said, his voice barely above a whisper. "I can tell she's planning her exit."

Alex had come to see me after a particularly difficult weekend with his wife, Emma. They'd been married for six years and had two young children. On the surface, things appeared stable—they had good jobs, a nice home, and presented as a happy family to the outside world. But inside, Alex was convinced his marriage was on the verge of collapse.

"What happened this weekend that made you so concerned?" I asked.

"She was distant all day Saturday. Barely talked to me. Then I found her on her laptop, and she closed it as soon as I walked in the room. Later, I saw a text notification on her phone from someone named

'Chris.' When I asked who that was, she just said, 'A colleague.' No details. And she's been taking more care with her appearance lately. New clothes. Different hairstyle."

He looked up at me, his face etched with certainty and pain. "She's having an affair. I know it. She's found someone else and she's planning to leave me."

"That sounds incredibly painful," I said. "I hear how real this feels to you. Before we go further, I'm curious. Have you talked with Emma directly about your concerns?"

He shook his head. "What's the point? She'll just deny it. And anyway, I don't want to look pathetic, begging her to stay when she's clearly made up her mind."

Here was a man suffering intensely, not from what was actually happening in his relationship, but from what he believed was happening. From the story his mind had created to explain a collection of ambiguous observations.

"Would you be willing to try something?" I asked. "Let's separate what you actually observed from the interpretation your mind has created about those observations."

Alex looked confused but nodded.

"Let's start with what you actually saw and heard—just the facts, without any interpretation about what they meant."

Alex thought for a moment. "Emma was quieter than usual on Saturday. When I walked into the room, she closed her laptop. She received a text from someone named Chris. When I asked who Chris was, she said 'A colleague.' She's bought some new clothes recently and changed her hairstyle."

"Good," I said. "Those are the observations. Now, what story has your mind created about what these observations mean?"

"That she's having an affair with this Chris person. That she's planning to leave me."

"And how certain do you feel about this interpretation?"

"One hundred percent," he said, then paused. "Well, maybe ninety percent. I guess I don't have absolute proof."

"What other interpretations might fit these same observations?" I asked.

He looked at me blankly. "What do you mean?"

"I mean, are there other possible explanations for the behaviors you observed that don't involve an affair?"

Alex was silent for a long moment. "I guess…maybe she's stressed about something else? Work has been difficult for her lately. But that doesn't explain closing the laptop when I came in, or being secretive about who Chris is."

"Maybe, maybe not. What if we explored some other possibilities? For instance, could she have been shopping for a surprise for you on the laptop? Could Chris be a female colleague? Could her change in appearance be for herself, not for someone else?"

For the first time since he'd arrived, a flicker of doubt crossed Alex's face. Not doubt about his relationship, but doubt about the certainty of his interpretation.

"I…I guess those are possibilities," he admitted. "But why wouldn't she just tell me if that were the case?"

"That's a great question to ask her directly," I said. "What I'm trying to show you is that while your interpretation feels completely true to you right now, it's still an interpretation, a story your mind has created to make sense of limited information. And when we mistake our interpretations for facts, we often create tremendous suffering for ourselves and our relationships."

Our minds are relentless meaning-making machines. We don't just observe reality; we interpret it, constantly and automatically. We take in sensory data—what we see, hear, feel, taste, and smell—and our minds immediately begin constructing a story to explain that data.

This meaning-making tendency is incredibly useful. It helps us navigate a complex world by identifying patterns, predicting outcomes, and making quick decisions. Without it, we'd be overwhelmed by the sheer volume of unprocessed sensory information.

But this same tendency creates problems when we forget we're doing it, when we mistake our interpretations for objective reality.

Alex wasn't simply observing his wife's behavior; he was interpreting it through the lens of his deepest fears and insecurities. His mind had taken a handful of ambiguous observations and woven them into a concrete story of betrayal and abandonment, a story that felt so real to him that he was ready to give up on his marriage without even having a conversation with his wife.

This gap between observation and interpretation exists in all our experiences, but it becomes particularly problematic in our relationships, where the stakes feel highest and our emotional triggers run deepest.

The interpretations or "stories" our minds create aren't random. They're shaped by our past experiences, our insecurities, our values, and our expectations. They're influenced by our mood, our physical state, and the broader context of our lives.

Alex's story was shaped by his early experiences of abandonment. His father had left the family when Alex was nine, disappearing with little explanation. His first serious girlfriend in college had cheated on him, blindsiding him with a breakup he never saw coming.

These experiences created a core narrative in Alex's mind: People leave. You can't trust the ones you love. You'll be abandoned again.

So when Emma showed behavior that could be interpreted in multiple ways, his mind immediately jumped to the interpretation that confirmed his core narrative. Not because it was the most likely explanation, but because it was the one his mind was primed to see.

We all have these core narratives that influence how we interpret the world. Some common ones include:

- "I'm not good enough so I must achieve" (leading to interpretations that others are judging us).
- "I'm not worth staying for so I can't trust others" (leading to interpretations that others are lying or betraying us).
- "I'm not good enough so I must be perfect" (leading to interpretations that any mistake means total failure).
- "I'm not worthy of care so I must be responsible for everyone else" (leading to interpretations that others' problems are our fault).

These core narratives don't just influence how we interpret isolated events; they shape our entire experience of reality. They determine what we notice, what we remember, and how we make decisions. They're like invisible scripts running in the background of our consciousness, influencing every aspect of our lives.

When we mistake our core narratives for reality, we pay a tremendous price:

1. **Suffering:** We experience emotional pain based not on what's actually happening, but on our interpretation of what's happening. Alex was in agony not because his wife was having an affair (she wasn't), but because he believed she was.

2. **Disconnection From Others:** We react to our interpretations rather than to the actual person in front of us, creating distance rather than connection. Alex was pulling away from Emma based on interpretations from his core narrative, making it even harder for them to communicate effectively.

3. **Self-Fulfilling Prophecies:** Interpretations based on our core narrative can shape our behavior in such a way that those behaviors can actually create the reality we fear. If Alex continued to act as if Emma was betraying him—becoming suspicious, accusatory, or withdrawn—he might have

damaged their relationship to the point where it actually did end.

4. **Disconnection From Truth and Reality:** When our interpretation is so strong that we see it as the only possible reality, we close ourselves off to other perspectives that could help us find the truth. Alex was ready to give up on his marriage based on interpretations from a core narrative that existed only in his mind.

The good news is that we can learn to notice the interpretations from our core narratives for what they are: interpretations, not facts, and most likely untrue interpretations. And in that noticing lies the possibility of freedom and choice.

THE PRACTICE

The practice of noticing your core narrative begins with learning to distinguish between direct observation and interpretation. Here's a process you can use:

IDENTIFY THE TRIGGER SITUATION

Start by identifying a situation that's causing you distress—an interaction, an event, or even a thought that's creating difficult emotions.

For Alex, the trigger situation was the combination of Emma's quietness, her closing the laptop, the text from "Chris," and her change in appearance.

LIST THE OBJECTIVE OBSERVATIONS

Next, write down only what you directly observed through your senses—what you saw, heard, felt, tasted, or smelled. Stick to descriptions that would be hard for someone else to dispute, like what a video camera might capture.

Alex's observations:

- Emma spoke less than usual on Saturday.
- She closed her laptop when I entered the room.
- She received a text from someone named Chris.
- When asked, she said Chris was "a colleague."
- She has bought new clothes recently.
- She has changed her hairstyle.

IDENTIFY YOUR INTERPRETATIONS

Your interpretations are the meaning you've assigned to these observations—your assumptions, beliefs, and conclusions about what they mean. Notice how your mind has gone beyond the direct evidence to create a story.

Alex's interpretations:

- Emma is hiding something from me.
- She's being secretive about her relationship with Chris.
- Chris is a man she's romantically involved with.
- She's changing her appearance to be attractive to him.
- She's planning to leave me.

NOTE THE GAP

Look at the difference between your observations and your interpretations. Notice how much of the story exists only in your mind, not in what you've actually observed.

For Alex, the gap was enormous. None of his observations directly indicated an affair or an intention to leave the marriage. His mind had created those possibilities and then treated them as certainties.

GENERATE ALTERNATIVE INTERPRETATIONS

Challenge yourself to come up with at least three other possible interpretations of the same observations. They don't have to be what you believe is happening—just what could be happening.

Alternative interpretations for Alex:

- Emma is planning a surprise for me and didn't want me to see.
- She's dealing with a stressful work situation that she's not ready to discuss.
- Chris is a female colleague who's going through a personal crisis.
- She's making changes to her appearance because it makes her feel good.
- She's been distant because she's not feeling well or is preoccupied with something unrelated to our relationship.

Test Your Interpretations (When Possible)

Look for ways to check your interpretations against reality. Ask yourself if these interpretations fit your core narrative. Ask direct questions of others involved, seek more information, or simply stay open to evidence that might contradict your story.

For Alex, this meant having an honest conversation with Emma about his concerns—not accusing her of having an affair, but sharing his experience and asking for her perspective.

In our next session, Alex came in with a completely different energy. The despair and resignation were gone, replaced by a mixture of relief and embarrassment.

"So, I talked to Emma," he said, shaking his head with a rueful smile. "Turns out she's been planning a surprise 40th birthday party for me. That's why she was on the laptop—looking at venues and creating a guest list. She closed it because she didn't want me to see."

"And Chris?" I asked.

"Christina. Her colleague from the marketing department who's helping her plan it because she threw a similar party for her husband last year."

"What about the new clothes and hairstyle?"

He laughed. "She got a bonus at work and decided to treat herself. Said she was tired of 'dressing like a mom' all the time and wanted to feel good about herself again."

"How are you feeling now?" I asked.

"Honestly? Like an idiot." He paused. "But also relieved. And… kind of amazed at how convinced I was of something that wasn't real at all. It felt so true."

"That's the power of our core narrative," I said. "It can lead us to make interpretations that can feel completely real even when they're not based in reality."

"The thing is," Alex continued, "when I started talking to Emma, I realized I'd been carrying this core narrative in my head for years. Little things she did or said that I interpreted as signs she was unhappy or restless. I've been living with this low-grade fear of being left for most of our marriage, and she had no idea."

This insight was the real breakthrough for Alex—not just recognizing that his specific interpretation in this instance was wrong, but understanding the power of his core narrative to cause interpretations that had been shaping the experience of his marriage for years.

"The conversation ended up being really good," he said. "Better than we've had in a long time. She told me she'd been feeling like I was pulling away, and she didn't know why. Like I wasn't fully present with her. And I realized that was me reacting to interpretations from my own core narrative. I've been creating distance because I was trying to protect myself from the abandonment I was sure was coming!"

THE RELATIONSHIP BETWEEN CORE NARRATIVE INTERPRETATIONS AND REALITY

It's important to understand that noticing your core narrative doesn't mean ruling out that some of the interpretations based on it could still be true. They just could be true for other reasons. Sometimes, people do have affairs. Sometimes, relationships do end.

But even when our interpretations turn out to be painful realities, we can handle them with conversation and connection rather than with reactivity and defensiveness, especially as we let go of our core narrative. We can embrace the inherent value of ourselves and the other person even if one of us has done something hurtful and wrong. Truth includes both our pain and our value.

The truth of our value helps us stand; the lies of our core narrative do not.

This willingness to hold our interpretations from our core narrative lightly doesn't mean we never act on them. It means we act on them appropriately, with awareness of their provisional nature. We might seek more information, ask clarifying questions, or express our concerns directly. But we do so from a place of openness rather than certainty.

When we begin to recognize our interpretations as interpretations rather than facts, especially when they come from our core narrative, we experience a significant shift in how we relate to ourselves and others:

Reduced Suffering: We no longer experience the full emotional impact of our worst-case scenarios as if they're already happening. Alex was able to move from despair to curiosity once he recognized his interpretations as interpretations.

Greater Connection: We can relate to the actual person in front of us, not the character in our core narrative. Alex and Emma had their most meaningful conversation in years once he stopped reacting to his interpretation of her.

More Truth and Reality: We open ourselves to multiple perspectives and interpretations that could help us find the actual truth, rather than being locked into a single interpretation as the only possibility. Alex was able to consider and explore alternative explanations for Emma's behavior, which led him to the truth.

Increased Freedom: We can choose how to respond based on a clearer perception of reality as we unmask and let go of our core narrative. Alex experienced new energy as he saw and let go of his core narrative that had been robbing him of the enjoyment of his marriage for years.

The gift of noticing your core narrative and learning to embrace your value is not a life free from interpretation (which is neither possible nor desirable), but the capacity to hold those interpretations more lightly, to see them as provisional rather than certain, to remain curious about what's actually happening rather than becoming trapped in a single narrative, and to pursue reality more confidently. That's the freedom Alex discovered, and it's available to all of us.

I was sitting with Elizabeth, a woman who'd spent decades building walls so high and thick that she couldn't see over them anymore. She'd come to me after her third divorce, exhausted and confused.

"I don't understand what's happening," she said, her voice cracking. "I'm a successful attorney. I can dismantle any opponent's argument in seconds. So why can't I figure out why my relationships keep failing?"

"Because you're using the same skill that makes you brilliant in court," I told her. "You're defending yourself from yourself."

She looked at me, puzzled. "What does that even mean?"

"To know yourself begins with mindfulness," I explained. "Not some complicated meditation practice, but simply noticing things. What are you thinking right now? What are you feeling in your body? What are you sensing about this situation? What judgments are you making?"

Elizabeth shifted uncomfortably. "I'm thinking this sounds like nonsense. I'm feeling irritated. I'm sensing that you're about to tell me something I don't want to hear, and I'm judging this entire process as a waste of time."

I smiled. "That's perfect. You just practiced mindfulness."

"So what?" she challenged back.

"So now ask yourself something deeper: What are your defenses? How do you protect yourself when you feel threatened?"

"I attack," she said without hesitation. "I find the weakness in the other person's position and I exploit it."

"Exactly. And you know why you choose that defense? Because you're good at it. We only choose defenses we're good at. That attack mode reveals your strength—your razor-sharp analytical mind."

Her posture softened slightly.

"But here's what most people miss," I continued. "Your defenses also reveal your weaknesses, your fears, your wounds, and the lies you believe about yourself."

"Such as?" she asked, her attorney's mind wanting specifics.

"Such as the belief that if you don't attack first, you'll be destroyed. The fear that if you're vulnerable even for a moment, someone will use it against you."

Tears filled her eyes. "In third grade," she whispered. "I told Jenny Myers I liked Brian Thompson, and by lunch, the entire school knew. They laughed at me for weeks."

"And what did you learn from that?" I asked gently.

"Never show weakness. Never admit what you really want."

"Those parts of you—the wounded parts, the frightened parts, the parts believing lies about your worth—they don't need defending. They need mending."

She wiped her eyes. "How do you mend something like that?"

"First by recognizing that who you really are isn't gone. You're just hurt and afraid. But you're still strong enough to take the risk of revealing yourself to someone safe." I leaned forward. "That's what you're doing right now."

Over the next few months, Elizabeth gradually lowered her defenses—first with me, then with a small group of carefully chosen friends, and eventually with a man she'd been dating cautiously.

"It's strange," she told me one day. "The less I defend, the stronger I feel."

"That's because your real self is emerging," I explained. "When we stop identifying with our wounds, our lies, and our fears, we start identifying with the truth, strength, and confidence that have always been there. We realize we've always been good and valuable; we just couldn't see it clearly."

Awareness of our value isn't some abstract psychological concept. It's the foundation for every meaningful connection we hope to have. When we don't know ourselves as valuable, we misuse our style of expressing ourselves, and that is like trying to build our relationships on quicksand. We shift and sink and wonder why nothing stands firm.

But when we take the brave step of turning our attention inward first—of noticing our thoughts, feelings, defenses, and deeper truths, especially about our value—we create solid ground. Not just for ourselves, but for anyone who wants to build something lasting with us.

CHAPTER 7

SPEAKING OUR ORIGINAL LANGUAGE

ROBERT AND JESSICA sat across from me, having been through three other therapists before landing in my office. Jessica turned to Robert and said, "I feel disconnected when you spend time on your phone. I mean, I know you really hate conversing and I get that, but I would really appreciate your considering me and my feelings. Because you don't, and it makes me feel disconnected." She glanced at me, confident she'd demonstrated perfect communication skills.

I let the moment settle before asking, "Where are you in that statement?"

She looked puzzled. "What do you mean? I used 'I feel' like we're supposed to."

Ahh…the communication pattern many of us learned, the infamous "I feel" statements. You know the ones I'm talking about. We think we're being emotionally intelligent when we say things like "I feel hurt when you act like a jerk, and I know you don't like me" or "I feel disrespected when you don't respond to my texts, and you simply think I'm too much."

But all too often, what's really happening is that we're using "I feel" as a Navy SEAL operation, sneaking behind enemy lines to launch an attack. We think we're being vulnerable, but it often lands as blame. We think we're expressing our emotions, but we're really just finding a veiled and socially acceptable way to criticize.

"Let's pause there," I told Jessica. "You're telling Robert that his behavior makes you feel a certain way. You've dressed it up in therapy clothes, but you're still talking about him."

This is where most of us get stuck. We think we're doing the work of emotional awareness because we've learned to say "I feel hurt" (accurate) instead of making accusations. We've been taught this is the gold standard of communication: leading with our emotions while pointing to someone else's actions. It's like trying to be vulnerable while wearing armor.

When you say, "I feel rejected when you work late, like you always do," you think you're talking about yourself, but they hear it as you making it about them. You're just doing it while wearing emotional camouflage. The emphasis is on them, not you. Then you're surprised when they respond defensively.

I looked at Jessica and said, "What if instead of telling Robert how his actions impact you, you got curious about what's happening inside of you? Not 'I feel hurt when YOU do X and all the things I believe about you,' rather, thinking to yourself, 'I'm noticing something's coming up for me right now. Let me understand what that is.'"

As Jessica finally started understanding what was going on inside of her, instead of launching into Robert, she began talking about herself. She verbalized her deep-seated fear of not being important enough and her struggle with feeling valued. She understood herself better. She understood her hurts. She communicated from her position, not his. In response, Robert's defensiveness melted away. He could hear her because she wasn't trying to make her feelings his responsibility to solve. She was truly sharing herself.

The difference is significant. One approach uses feelings as evidence in a case we're building against someone else. The other requires the real courage of looking inward first, understanding ourselves, and sharing that understanding—without making it about anyone else.

This isn't just semantics or therapy jargon. It's about whether we're truly willing to know ourselves, to sit with our own experience before we try to change someone else's behavior. When we do this work, we stop using "I feel" statements as sophisticated weapons and start using them as genuine windows into ourselves.

Let me tell you about another couple I work with. He's a litigating attorney who talks like a nail gun. Every word is precision-aimed, trying to pin down exact meanings. His wife? She is riddled with anxiety and talks backward, starting at the end of her thoughts and working her way to the beginning because she is gripped with fear of speaking.

I watched them in session one day and finally said to him, "It seems like you're trying to nail her down for what she means." Then I looked at her and said, "And you, madam, you tend to talk backward. I understand that because sometimes I explain things backward too. I start up here in the atmosphere and sometimes struggle to touch the earth."

But here's what's really going on: He's firing questions like a nail gun because he's terrified of uncertainty. If he can just get her to be clear enough, precise enough, maybe then he'll feel secure. Meanwhile, she's so worried about getting it wrong that she circles around her points, trying to find the perfect way in.

However, put them together and you have conversations that look like this:

> "You never help with the kids' homework!"
> "Well, you're always criticizing how I do it!"
> "You're just too sensitive!"
> "You're impossible to please!"

Sound familiar? Maybe your version isn't about homework. Maybe it's about money, or in-laws, or who forgot to buy milk—again. But the dance is the same: You, you, you, you, you."

One day, I stopped them mid-argument. "Lisa, what are you feeling right now?"

"I'm feeling like he's never going to understand me," she said.

"That's about him. What are you feeling?"

She paused. "I…I feel scared."

Mark's head snapped up. This was new.

"Tell me more," I encouraged.

"I feel scared that nothing I do will ever be enough. That I'll always be wrong. Maybe I am as stupid as I felt in school."

Mark's face softened. "I don't think you're stupid," he said quietly.

"I believe that," she replied. "But that's where I go when I get rapid-fire questions directed at me. I freeze up. My brain stops working. Just like it did in school."

For the first time in weeks, they were talking to each other instead of at each other. Why? Because they'd switched from the language of "you" to the language of "I."

Here's what I want you to understand: Most of us are walking around speaking a second language without realizing our native tongue is still available to us. We're so fluent in "you" statements that we've forgotten how to speak from "I."

Let me tell you why this is so hard.

I had another client—let's call her Samantha—who spent three sessions telling me everything her husband was doing wrong. When I finally got her to talk about herself, she burst into tears.

"If I say what I'm really feeling," she admitted, "and he still doesn't change…then what? Then I have to face that maybe this isn't fixable. Maybe I'm not enough. Maybe we're not enough."

Bingo.

Remember Mike, our client from Chapter 2, who was expected to be "The One Who Knows" in his career? The one who couldn't tell people how he felt about his cancer? Here's what he said when he finally started speaking his truth: "I'm terrified. Not just of dying, but of being out of control. Of being vulnerable. Of needing help."

That's the real language of self.—not "I feel" disguised as "I feel this about YOU." "I feel" is about what you feel. It's about helping you better understand you, not them.

LEARNING TO SPEAK

So how do we learn this new language? The same way we learn any language—with practice, with patience, and with a lot of awkward moments along the way.

I had a client, Stephanie, whose mom had mastered the art of creating chaos around special occasions, especially at Christmas. Every year, like clockwork, she'd wait until the last possible minute to ask, "What do you want me to get the kids for Christmas? I need to know by this evening! Please do not keep me waiting. I am trying to finish my shopping. Get back with me within the hour."

Stephanie would feel this immediate burden, this pressure to drop everything and figure it out. And every time she'd tell me about it, her voice would tighten with frustration: "I hate it because she always waits till the last minute to ask me. It's such a burden on me to try to figure out what she can get the kids with the looming deadline."

One day, after hearing this pattern for the umpteenth time, I asked her, "If I spit on my hand and stuck it out to shake your hand, would you shake it?"

"Oh God, no!" she recoiled.

"Then why do you keep shaking hers?"

Stephanie stared at me, confused. "I'm not… I mean, that's different. I should just get over it. I'll get back to her later."

"No, no," I said. "You're still taking the hand. When she says, 'What do you want me to get the kids for Christmas? Call me back immediately. Don't keep me waiting,' you might say, 'Oh gosh, what did you have planned?'"

"Okay, but she's going to say nothing," Stephanie replied.

"Exactly. Then what do you say?"

"Well, I guess I just have to tell her I'll get back to her later."

"No, you're still taking the spit-ridden hand. The way you let it go is to say, 'I'm sure you'll find something great to give them.'"

Stephanie's eyes widened. "But then I have to hear my kids bemoan whatever she gives them. And hear her upset that I held up her shopping quest."

"Wait, wait, wait—now you're taking multiple spit-ridden hands too. You're either choosing to feel angry and overlooked while trying to control the environment, or you're choosing to let go of control. But here's the question: When you try to control everything, who do you lose control of?"

She sat with that for a moment. "Me," she finally said.

"Exactly. You either give up control of yourself and stay angry, or you stay in control of you and let others handle their own choices."

This is what most people miss about boundaries: They think setting them means being mean or uncaring. But boundaries aren't about other people at all. They're about you, about recognizing what you can and cannot hold without losing yourself in the process.

When Stephanie learned to say, "I'm sure you'll find something wonderful," she wasn't being unkind. She was simply refusing to take responsibility for someone else's choices. And yes, sometimes her mom gave gifts the kids didn't love. But Stephanie learned that she didn't have to manage everyone's feelings about that either.

That's what showing up really means—not being available for every demand, but being present with your own perspective. It means being willing to let others make their own choices while you stay who you really are by keeping your own boundaries. Sometimes, the kindest thing you can do, for yourself and others, is to stop trying to control situations that aren't yours to control in the first place.

Stephanie realized where she was in the situation. She realized that she had been trying to control her mom's view of her by never saying "no." She saw herself, and that is what allowed her to give up her control and set her boundaries instead.

Boundaries aren't about controlling others; they are about expressing and protecting you. They are invitations for others to know you and have the chance to help you if they so choose. (They are also guardrails to help you not get pulled back into the control illusion.)

Finally, boundaries are about using your "I" language effectively.

I had a client once who kept saying to her son, "You can't talk to me that way!" Guess what? He could and he did. When Mom used her "I" language, she said: "I won't continue conversations where I am being spoken to disrespectfully." And guess what? She didn't. "You" language tries to control others; "I" language expresses the control you already have over you.

Before trying to change your boundaries, make sure you are in touch with who you are in the moment. Here's something to try next time you feel not fully present within yourself, and perhaps even begin spiraling from anxiety or fear: Check your anchor.

One of my clients, Ethan, recently shared a story that illuminated this perfectly. His grandmother, who lives with his parents, had sent him an unexpected gift of money. A kind gesture, simple enough. My client responded with a text that said how grateful he was for it, but he never received a response to his text. As a result, my client felt that old, familiar weight in his chest.

"I bet you my thank-you wasn't enough," Ethan told me. "My mom's probably looking at it, my grandmother's probably looking at it, both of them thinking about how ungrateful I am because I didn't use exactly the right words, didn't respond in exactly the right way. Didn't live up to what they would want me to say."

"Where's your focus right now? Internal or external?" I asked him.

He looked confused, so I continued. "Picture an anchor. In this moment, where is it dropped? Is it planted firmly within you, grounded in your own experience? Or is it cast out there, hooked into their potential disappointment, their imagined judgments?"

His eyes widened with recognition. "It's completely tangled up in their reactions. I'm not even thinking about how I genuinely feel about the gift. I'm just trying to avoid their disapproval."

This is what I mean by checking where you are anchored, internally or externally. In any interaction, especially with people who have historically held power over your sense of self-worth, pause and visualize your anchor. Ask yourself:

- Is it rooted in someone else's expected reaction?
- Is it caught on past patterns of disappointment?
- Is it thrown out desperately seeking approval?
- Or is it grounded firmly in your perspective?

If your anchor is cast out into someone else's waters—their opinions, their potential reactions, their imagined judgments—pull it back. Visualize yourself hauling it in, feeling its weight, and dropping it back down within yourself.

For my client, this meant taking a breath and asking himself: "How do I genuinely feel about this gift? What is my authentic response?" Only then could he feel at peace with the thank-you message he wrote that came from a place of true gratitude rather than fear of judgment.

The point isn't to ignore others' feelings or reactions. It's about making sure you're responding from a grounded place rather than letting old patterns and feared disappointments drive your behavior.

Your anchor can be out there, thrown into choppy waters of others' opinions, getting yanked around by every wave of potential disapproval. Or it can be dropped deep within you, holding you steady regardless of the surface storms.

The choice is yours. But you have to check first to know where it's actually planted.

The goal isn't to never care what others think. It's to make sure your responses come from a place of being anchored in yourself rather than desperately trying to avoid the storms of others' reactions.

The ultimate goal in all that we're doing with learning to show up as who we truly are and be present isn't to become a Zen master who never gets rattled. It's to build better connections while staying true to yourself, learning to dance with others without losing your own rhythm.

Your relationships with others are laboratories for growth, not battlegrounds for control. Every interaction is an opportunity to understand yourself better and to practice showing up as your authentic self while allowing others to do the same. It's about learning how to recover faster, notice sooner, and choose differently when you can.

Some days, you'll nail it. Some days, you'll forget everything and react like you always have. That's okay. The practice isn't in doing it perfectly. It's in coming back, again and again, to you.

PRACTICE

Use "I" language to express who you are and where you are in situations. Think of something that's bothering you right now. Maybe it's something someone did or didn't do. Maybe it's a situation at work. Maybe it's a family dynamic.

First, write down how you'd normally express this. Be honest—no one's going to see this but you.

Now, let's translate it:

1. Circle every "you" statement.
2. What are you feeling when this happens?
3. What does this situation bring up in you?
4. What do you need? (To reveal an emotion? To check your hypothesis? To make a request? A refusal?)
5. How can you express this using "I"?

I watched Emma do this exercise in real time:

Original Version: "You're always on your phone when the kids are around. You don't care about the example you're setting. You're making it impossible for me to parent effectively."

Translated Version: "I feel lonely when technology takes center stage in our family time. I'm unsettled about the patterns we're setting. I need us to be partners in this."

Same concern, completely different impact.

Remember Rachel and Tom from Chapter 1? Here's how I worked with Rachel on translating her language:

"He doesn't care about me" became "I feel unimportant."

"He's choosing those videos over me" became "I feel rejected."

"He needs to stop lying" became "I need to trust and feel safe."

Each translation moved her closer to herself, closer to what was actually happening in her heart. And here's the fascinating thing—the moment she started speaking from this more vulnerable place, Tom stopped staring at the floor. He looked up. He leaned in.

"I never wanted you to feel unimportant," he said, his voice cracking. "I'm ashamed. I don't know how to face you when I fail."

Now we were getting somewhere.

Here's what happens when we learn to speak from the self:

1. **We Learn About Ourselves:** When John finally spoke about his fears instead of what his mother wouldn't do, he discovered what was really driving his anxiety. We often, unknowingly, push people to care for our feelings rather than being aware of and taking care of these emotions for ourselves.

2. **We Create Space for Real Connection:** When Jessica shared her fear instead of her accusations, Robert could finally see her instead of just defending against her. She was honoring herself and Robert by giving him a chance to understand her fears as opposed to her criticizing Robert.

3. **We Take Our Power Back:** When Rachel learned to say "I feel unimportant" instead of "You don't care about me," she moved from powerless to powerful. She couldn't control Tom's behavior, but she could own her experience. She was showing Tom how things were impacting her rather than demanding from him.

4. **We Give Others Permission to Do the Same:** When Emma spoke authentically about motherhood, Josh could drop his defenses and actually hear her. Vulnerability often leads to intimacy. In this case, it was an open door to really understand each other's fears as opposed to the fears being a stumbling block to their closeness.

Here's the thing about learning a new language: There's usually an awkward stage. That period where you're translating everything in your head before you speak, where you stumble over words, where you fall back into old patterns when you're tired or stressed. It can feel like you're exposed, so it's easier to run back to the safety of "you" statements and finger-pointing.

That's okay. That's normal. That's part of the process.

My client, Jenny, was trying to have a difficult conversation with her mother. She'd practiced her "I" statements. She was ready. Then her mom said something triggering, and Jenny went right back to "You always do this! You never listen!"

When she came to my office, she was devastated. "I failed," she said.

"No," I told her, "you practiced. There's a difference."

People don't transform overnight. But every time you choose to speak from "I" and stay present instead of disappearing, you show up and so does your true style. That is powerful.

You also are offering the opportunity to build a new pattern with someone. If they take the opportunity, it can create a new dance that will be more enjoyable for both of you. You send the invitation, but it is still up to them to take it. Whether they do or not, you will still be dancing from your side. You can take the first step and see what happens. It will be awkward, but also powerful.

HOW WE ANSWER THE QUESTION

CHAPTER 8

FINDING YOUR OWN POWER

THE MOST COMMON complaint I hear as a therapist is that people feel disconnected from others. They desperately want meaningful relationships but find themselves in patterns that leave them feeling alone, misunderstood, or resentful. They feel powerless to change. What most don't realize is that the disconnection from others stems from a disconnection from themselves and their power.

I sat across from Elena, an accomplished mother of four who, despite her many accomplishments, felt her life was spiraling out of control. Her teenage son was struggling with substance use, her aging parents needed increasing care, and her marriage was strained under the weight of it all.

"I'm doing everything I can," she said, her voice breaking. "I've found the best treatment program for my son. I've researched every care option for my parents. I've scheduled weekly date nights with my husband. But nothing's getting better. In fact, everything feels worse."

She looked at me, desperation in her eyes. "What am I doing wrong?"

"It sounds like you're trying to control what can't be controlled," I said gently.

She stared at me blankly. "What do you mean? I'm just trying to fix the problems."

"That's exactly it," I replied. "You're approaching these situations as problems you can solve through effort, research, and planning. But your son's recovery isn't something you can control. Your parents' aging isn't something you can control. Your husband's feelings aren't something you can control."

"So I'm just supposed to give up?" she asked, anger edging into her voice.

"Not at all," I said. "But there's a difference between caring about these situations and thinking you can control them. When we confuse the two, we create tremendous suffering for ourselves and often make things worse for everyone involved."

Look, I know this sounds like I'm telling you something simple, but trust me—this understanding of where you end and the environment begins? It's probably the most crucial distinction you'll ever make in your expedition toward authentic connection.

THE MISPLACED POWER PROBLEM

Many of us operate with a fundamentally flawed mental model of power. We believe power is about control. It is not. It is about influence. When we show up as ourselves, we have influence. Who we are and how we express ourselves can be powerful. When we show up to control others, we have neither influence (at least the kind we want) nor power.

One of my favorite illustrations of an accurate view of power comes from the ancient story of David and Goliath. Most people know the basic outline: A young shepherd boy defeats a fearsome giant warrior using only a sling and stone. But what's often missed is the lesson about power embedded in the story.

When David was called on to fight Goliath, what did he do first? He tried to put on King Saul's armor, essentially taking on someone else's identity. He tried to become what he thought a warrior should be—armored, sword-wielding, imposing.

But what happened? It was too heavy. He couldn't move in it. The armor was built for someone else's body, someone else's way of fighting. So what did David do instead?

He used a slingshot. David dropped the false identity and embraced who he truly was: a shepherd who knew how to use a slingshot with deadly accuracy. When he went down to the stream to select stones, he was returning to himself, to his own strengths, to his own way of being.

The miracle isn't that a small stone somehow magically defeated a giant. When wielded by someone skilled, a slingshot can propel a stone at the velocity of a .45 caliber bullet. The miracle is that David fought as David amid great pressure to fight as someone else. And he won!

If David had shown up as anyone other than himself that day, he would have died. And the same is true for us. When we try to fight our battles without being ourselves, maybe wearing someone else's identity, using someone else's weapons, we're setting ourselves up for defeat.

This is the truth: We must know ourselves before we can effectively engage with others. When we don't know ourselves or try to be someone else to fight our battles, we become weighed down and ineffective. But when we embrace our authentic selves—with all our unique strengths and ways of being—we find our real power has been inside of us all along.

Elena's "armor" was the belief that if she just found the right treatment program, made the right parenting decisions, and said the right things, she could control her son's recovery. This armor wasn't just ineffective; it was crushing her beneath its weight.

MINDFULNESS: DISCOVERING OUR OWN POWER

When most people hear "mindfulness," they think of meditation apps or breathing exercises. But at its core, mindfulness is simply the practice of paying attention to what's actually happening, rather than what we think should be happening or what we fear might be going to happen.

1. True mindfulness involves three essential components:
    - Present-Moment Awareness: Noticing what's happening inside and outside of you right now, rather than dwelling in the past or anxiously anticipating the future. Where are you?
    - Non-Judgment: Observing without immediately labeling experiences as good or bad, right or wrong.
    - Value Awareness: Noticing that you matter, you count even without doing anything.

    This third component—value—is crucial for helping us stay present with what we are experiencing in the present moment. We will have the powerful experience of feeling difficult feelings and knowing that we are okay at the same time. This is the source of our power. This helps us stand in any battle.

2. Now you can remember the qualities that define you: personality, strengths, values, style, etc. Who are you? When you see what you are equipped with, you will be able to show up with it and not with something you think you are supposed to show up with. (In the last section of this book, we will look more closely at the qualities that make you who you are.)

3. And finally, you can choose to respond out of who you are with expressions of care, support, and even giving your perspective when asked. Like David, we can craft our responses out of who we are. We can choose our desired outcome for

our own behavior, not for the other person's. When we show up with our authentic self, we have great power.

POWER LEAKS

Power leaks happen whenever we take our eyes off of ourselves and put them on external situations or other people. The personal power we were holding begins to leak as we make the mistake of thinking we can best take care of our needs and others' needs by using control. We not only have lost our power of influence, but we have put ourselves at the mercy of how others respond to our control—and they are in control of how they respond to our control. This is how we give up the power of influence for the illusion of control.

Here is what power leaks sound like:

- "You make me so angry!"
- "If only they would change, I'd be happy."
- "I have to do this because they expect it."

No matter how good our control tactics (guilt, pity, placating, etc.), we are out of power.

When we clearly discern what is and isn't ours to control, we can place our energy and attention where they can make a difference, rather than exhausting ourselves trying to change what can't be changed.

Imagine you're at the beach, holding a beach ball underwater. What happens when you try to keep it submerged? It takes constant effort and attention. The moment you relax your vigilance or strength, the ball pops up. The harder you push it down, the more forcefully it rebounds when your grip slips.

This is what happens when we try to control what isn't ours to control. Whether it's attempting to manage others' perceptions of us, trying to force a specific outcome, or believing we can prevent painful emotions through sheer will, we're holding a beach ball underwater—expending tremendous energy on an impossible task.

The alternative isn't to let go of caring or to become passive. It's to redirect our energy toward what we can actually influence:

- Instead of trying to control others' behavior, we can choose our responses.
- Instead of trying to ensure a specific outcome, we can focus on our contribution.
- Instead of trying to avoid difficult emotions, we can develop our capacity to be with them skillfully.

This redirection—this proper placement of our power—creates the conditions for peace and effective action.

MAPPING YOUR CONTROL BOUNDARIES

Between what we can control (our own responses) and what we can't control (most everything else) lies an important middle territory: what we can influence but not directly control.

For example, while you can't control how others perceive you, you can influence those perceptions through how you show up and communicate. While you can't control whether a project succeeds, you can influence its trajectory through your contributions and leadership. While you can't control whether someone changes a problematic behavior, you can influence the conditions that make change more or less likely.

One powerful practice for developing this discernment is mapping your control boundaries. This involves systematically examining different areas of your life and sorting what aspects are within your control, what aspects are within your influence (but not control), and what aspects are outside both your control and influence.

Understanding this domain of influence—and its limitations—is crucial for effective action without the frustration of attempted control.

Here's what this mapping process looks like for Elena, our dedicated mom client:

Within Her Control

- her own behavior and responses to her son
- the boundaries she set around what behavior she would and wouldn't accept
- how she cared for her own well-being during this crisis
- the resources and support she offered
- her decisions about when to help and when to step back

Within Her Influence (But Not Control)

- the treatment options available to her son
- the family environment and its impact on her son's choices
- the information and perspective she shared with her son
- the consequences her son experienced for his choices

Outside Her Control

- her son's decisions about substance use
- her son's readiness to change
- the timeline of her son's recovery process
- whether treatment would be effective
- her son's thoughts, feelings, and ultimate choices

This mapping process didn't diminish Elena's love or commitment to her son. Instead, it helped her redirect her energy from the futile attempt to control his recovery to the areas where she could truly make a difference: maintaining her own well-being, setting clear and consistent boundaries, offering support without enabling, and showing up authentically in the relationship.

Over time, this shift allowed her to be more effectively present for her son while reducing her own suffering. And by acknowledging the limits of her control, she became more impactful in the areas where she did have influence.

There's a paradoxical freedom that comes from accepting what we can't control. Instead of exhausting ourselves trying to manage the unmanageable, we can redirect that energy toward what we can affect.

Accepting the limits of her control didn't mean Elena cared less or did less. In fact, it allowed her to care more effectively and to take more impactful actions. She stopped trying to force her son into recovery, which was outside of her control and instead focused on maintaining clear boundaries, taking care of her own well-being, and being authentically present when he was ready to engage.

This acceptance isn't resignation or passivity. It's a clear-eyed recognition of reality that allows for more effective and authentic engagement with life's challenges. It's the wisdom to know, as the Serenity Prayer suggests, what we can change, what we can't change, and the difference between the two.

THE PRACTICE

Developing this discernment isn't a one-time achievement but an ongoing practice.

Here's a simple daily reflection that can help cultivate this essential wisdom:

1. **Notice Areas of Tension or Struggle:** What do you feel? Where do you feel frustrated, anxious, or stuck? These emotions often signal places where you're attempting to control what can't be controlled.

2. **Ask Clarifying Questions:** In this situation, what aspects are within your control? What aspects can you influence but not control? What aspects are beyond both your control and influence?

3. **Place Your Energy Intentionally:** Focus your attention and effort on what you can control, use your influence wisely where it exists, and practice acceptance of what you can neither control nor influence.

4. **Observe the Results:** Notice how this proper placement of power affects your well-being, effectiveness, and relationships.

Over time, this practice builds the "muscle" of discernment, the ability to quickly and accurately distinguish between what is and isn't yours to control.

Perhaps the most important benefit of properly placed power is its impact on our relationships. When we try to control others—their choices, behaviors, feelings, or perceptions—we create disconnection.

Think about how you feel when someone tries to control you—when they pressure you to make certain choices, tell you how you should feel, or attempt to manage your behavior through manipulation, criticism, or force. Do you feel closer to that person? More trusting? More open? Probably not.

The same principle applies when we try to control others. Even when our intentions are good, even when we're trying to help or protect, attempting to control what isn't ours to control damages connection rather than enhancing it.

I worked with a mother who was desperately trying to control her adult daughter's life choices, believing she knew what would make her daughter happy. The more she tried to control—through advice, criticism, emotional pressure, and financial leverage—the more her daughter pulled away. Their relationship had deteriorated to brief, superficial interactions punctuated by conflict.

Through our work together, the mother began to recognize that her daughter's life choices weren't hers to control. She could offer perspective when asked, express her caring, and be available for support, but the decisions themselves belonged to her daughter.

As she released her grip on trying to control her daughter's path, something remarkable happened: Their relationship began to heal. Without the constant pressure to conform to her mother's vision, the daughter began to reach out more, to share more of her experience, to seek connection rather than avoid it.

This is the gift of properly placed power in relationships: When we stop trying to control others and instead focus on how we show up, we create the conditions for authentic connection rather than control-based disconnection.

Knowing where you end and the environment begins—understanding what is and isn't within your control—is perhaps the most essential wisdom for both personal well-being and meaningful relationships.

When we place our power where it actually exists—in our own responses, choices, and ways of showing up—we simultaneously free ourselves from the exhausting attempt to control the uncontrollable and empower ourselves to make a genuine difference where we can.

Like David facing Goliath, we recognize that we can't control the size of the giants we face or the conventional wisdom about how to fight them. What we can control is whether we show up authentically, using our true strengths rather than trying to be someone we're not.

Notice where you're placing your power, and adjust accordingly. Release the exhausting grip on what you can't control and place your energy where it can make a difference: in your own responses, choices, and ways of showing up to the challenges life inevitably brings.

In this proper placement of power, you'll find not just greater peace and effectiveness, but the foundation for authentic connection with both yourself and others. And isn't that what we're all after in the end?

"I can't do this anymore," Megan said, sinking into the couch in my office. Her voice was barely above a whisper, but I could hear the resolve beneath the exhaustion. "These family dinners are killing me."

Megan was thirty-four, successful in her career as a marketing executive, married to a supportive husband, and by all external measures, thriving. Yet every Wednesday evening, she found herself sitting at her mother's dining room table, feeling like she was shrinking back into an insecure teenager.

"Tell me about last night," I prompted.

She took a deep breath. "It started the moment I walked in. Mom looked me up and down and said, 'Oh, you're wearing that to dinner?' Then my sister arrived with her kids, and Mom couldn't stop praising how well-behaved they are, with this look at me—" Megan's eyes welled up. "We don't have children yet. She knows we've been trying for three years."

I nodded, giving her space to continue.

"Then during dinner, she brought up my cousin's new promotion, asking if I was 'ever going to move up' at my company. When I mentioned the project I'm leading, she changed the subject." Megan wiped at a tear. "I'm thirty-four years old, and I left feeling like I was nothing."

"And this happens every Wednesday?" I asked.

"Like clockwork. Sometimes, it's worse. Sometimes, it's just a steady drip of little comments. But I always leave feeling...diminished."

"What keeps you going back?" I asked gently.

Megan looked startled by the question. "It's family dinner. Everyone goes. My sister, her husband, their kids, my aunt sometimes. It's just what we do."

"Says who?"

She blinked. "My mom would be devastated if I stopped coming."

"And that would be terrible because…?"

"Because I'm responsible for her feelings," Megan said automatically, then paused. "Wait, that's not right, is it?"

I smiled slightly. "What do you think?"

Megan was illustrating a "power leak," the loss of personal power when she unwittingly gave into the control illusion. When she thought she could control her mother's emotions, Megan experienced the results of powerlessness:

1. She prioritized family expectations over her own well-being.
2. She tolerated behavior that diminished her.
3. She showed up again and again to an environment that left her feeling depleted.

The result? A weekly emotional drainage that affected not just Wednesday evenings, but cast a shadow over her entire week—not only dreading the upcoming dinner, but then having to process the aftermath.

In all my years of practice, I've seen this pattern emerge more frequently than almost any other. We give away our power in small moments, seemingly inconsequential decisions, and subtle shifts in our behavior to accommodate others. Over time, these power leaks drain our energy, confidence, and ability to show up as our authentic selves.

THE SOURCE OF POWER LEAKS

At our next session, I asked Megan to tell me more about the history of these family dinners.

"They started after my dad died," she explained. "I was twenty-two. Mom was devastated, and my sister suggested weekly dinners to keep the family connected. At first, it felt good—like we were honoring Dad by staying close."

"When did they start feeling different?" I asked.

Megan thought for a moment. "About five years ago. My sister had her first child, and suddenly everything shifted. Mom's whole world became about her grandchildren, and nothing I did seemed to matter anymore."

"And before your dad died, what was your relationship with your mother like?"

"He was the buffer," Megan said without hesitation. "When he was alive, he'd step in when Mom got critical. He'd say things like, 'Barbara, our daughter is doing just fine,' or he'd change the subject. Without him there…" She trailed off.

"The criticism comes directly at you," I finished for her.

She nodded. "And there's no one to stop it."

"No one except you," I said quietly.

Megan looked up, startled. "What do you mean?"

"I mean that while your father was alive, he was taking responsibility for managing the dynamic between you and your mother. He was using his power to create boundaries. When he died, that responsibility didn't automatically transfer to you—and you have never picked it up."

"I never thought about it that way," Megan said slowly.

"Here's what I'm curious about," I continued. "When your mother makes these comments that leave you feeling diminished, what do you do?"

"I usually just sit there and take it," she admitted. "Sometimes, I make a joke to lighten the mood. Once in a while, I'll change the subject like Dad used to do."

"Have you ever directly addressed it with her? Said something like, 'Mom, all of these comments on my clothes make me feel so judged'?"

Megan shook her head vehemently. "No way. That would create a whole scene. She'd get defensive, probably cry, and then my sister would text me later saying I upset Mom."

"So you protect your mother from the consequences of her behavior, and then your sister protects her too," I observed. "Meanwhile, who's protecting you?"

The question hung in the air between us. Megan's eyes filled with tears again, but these were different—not tears of hurt, but of recognition.

"Nobody," she whispered. "Nobody is protecting me."

What Megan was describing is common in family systems. After her father died, the family reorganized itself around an unspoken agreement: Megan's mother's emotional comfort was the priority, and everyone else adjusted accordingly. In this system, Megan's role was to absorb whatever came her way without complaint, to be the "good daughter" who didn't make waves. She didn't ask to be given control of her mother's emotions; it was just given to her.

This is how power leaks often work. They're not usually dramatic moments where someone forcibly takes our power. Instead, they're subtle agreements we make, often unconsciously, to give away pieces of ourselves for the sake of maintaining a relationship or keeping peace in a system. But it's an illusion. We simply do not have control over the emotions of others.

For Megan, these control agreements looked like:

- "I will tolerate being diminished because addressing it would upset my mother."

- "My feelings matter less than maintaining harmony."
- "My sister's choices (having children) are more valid than mine."
- "I am responsible for managing my mother's emotions by being who she wants me to be."

Each of these agreements to control her mom's emotions was a hole through which Megan's power steadily drained. And as long as these leaks remained, she would continue to show up to those Wednesday dinners, week after week, feeling smaller each time.

In our third session, Megan came in looking both anxious and determined.

"I've been thinking about what you said," she began. "About how no one is protecting me. And I realized something: I'm thirty-four years old. Maybe I shouldn't be looking for someone to protect me. Maybe that's my job now."

I smiled. "That's a powerful realization."

"So I've decided not to go to dinner tonight," she continued. "I called my mom this morning and told her I wouldn't be there."

"How did she respond?"

Megan grimaced. "About how you'd expect. First, she wanted to know if I was sick. When I said no, she asked what was so important that I would miss family dinner. When I just said I needed a break, she got quiet, then said, 'I see where I stand in your priorities,' and hung up."

"That sounds difficult," I acknowledged. "How are you feeling about it?"

"Guilty," Megan admitted immediately. "Like I'm a terrible daughter. But also…" She paused, searching for the right word. "Relieved. Like I can breathe a little deeper today knowing I don't have to gear myself up for tonight."

"Both of those feelings make sense," I said. "The guilt comes from breaking an unspoken agreement that's been in place for years. The relief comes from honoring your own needs for the first time in a long time."

"My phone's been buzzing all morning," she continued. "My sister has texted three times asking what's going on. I haven't answered yet."

"What would you like to say to her?"

Megan thought for a moment. "The truth, I guess. That the dinners have become stressful for me, and I need some space."

"That sounds reasonable." I nodded. "And what if she gets upset too?"

"That's what I'm afraid of," Megan admitted. "I don't want to hurt anyone. I just need to not feel awful every Wednesday."

"Megan," I said gently, "this is an important moment. You're worried about hurting your mother's and sister's feelings by making a choice that protects your own well-being. What does that tell you about how power is distributed in your family?"

She was quiet for a long time. "It tells me that their feelings are allowed to matter more than mine."

"And who allowed that arrangement?"

Another long pause.

"I did," she finally said. "I've been allowing it."

"Exactly," I smiled. "Which means you can un-allow it too."

RECLAIMING YOUR POWER

This is the first step in reclaiming your power: recognizing that you've been giving it away. Not because you're weak or flawed, but because you were operating under a set of assumptions about your role and responsibilities in relation to others.

In Megan's case, she had assumed several things:

1.   Her presence at family dinners was nonnegotiable.

2. Her mother's happiness was her responsibility.
3. Saying "no" was an act of cruelty rather than self-care.
4. Her needs mattered less than the needs of the family system.

None of these assumptions were true, but they felt true because they had been reinforced over years of interaction. Challenging them felt threatening, not just to the relationship, but to Megan's very identity as a "good daughter."

This is where people get stuck. They intellectually understand that they're giving away their power, but emotionally, they can't bear the perceived consequences of reclaiming it. The fear of disapproval, conflict, or abandonment keeps them locked in patterns that drain their energy and diminish their sense of self.

The following week, Megan returned looking both exhausted and somehow lighter.

"It's been a hell of a week," she said, settling into the now-familiar couch. "My mom called every day, alternating between guilt trips and cold silence. My sister showed up at my house on Friday night to 'check on me' and spent an hour telling me how selfish I was."

"That sounds intense," I acknowledged. "How did you handle it?"

A small smile appeared. "Better than I would have a month ago. I kept reminding myself that their reactions belong to them, not to me. I didn't argue or defend. I just kept saying that I needed some time and space, and that I still love them but need to take care of myself too."

"And how did that go?"

"Mom hung up on me twice," Megan said with a wry laugh. "My sister eventually stormed out saying I'd 'changed' and not for the better. But you know what? I didn't cave. I didn't promise to come back to dinners. I didn't apologize for needing space."

"That's significant," I noted. "In the past, would you have apologized just to keep the peace?"

"Absolutely." She nodded. "I would have been back at that dinner table the very next week, pretending everything was fine."

"And how are you feeling about your decision now, a week later?"

Megan thought for a moment. "Still guilty sometimes. Still worried about the long-term impact on my relationships. But also…stronger. Like I've finally stood up for myself in a meaningful way."

"What's been the hardest part?" I asked.

"The hardest part," she said slowly, "is accepting that I can't make everyone happy. That preserving myself means some people will be upset with me, and I have to be okay with that."

"That's a powerful realization," I said. "Many people never get there. They spend their lives trying to manage other people's perceptions and reactions, and in the process, they lose themselves."

Megan nodded. "I think that's what was happening to me. Every Wednesday, I'd leave a little piece of myself at that dinner table. Eventually, there wouldn't have been anything left."

Power leaks don't just affect how we feel in the moment; they shape our identity over time. When we repeatedly silence our own voice to amplify others, ignore our own needs to meet others' demands, or shrink ourselves to make others comfortable, we internalize the message that our power doesn't belong to us.

The good news is that we can reclaim this power through conscious choice and consistent practice. For Megan, saying "no" to some of the weekly dinners was just the beginning. The real work came in holding her boundary in the face of pushback and sitting with the discomfort of others' disappointment without taking responsibility for it.

Over the next several months, Megan continued to work on plugging her power leaks, not just with her family but in other areas of her life as well. She noticed how she would automatically apologize at work for expressing an opinion, how she would exhaust herself trying to anticipate her husband's needs before her own, how she would agree to social engagements she didn't want to attend just to avoid disappointing someone.

Each time she identified a leak, she would practice a new response, one that honored her needs and values while still maintaining connection with others. It wasn't about becoming selfish or uncaring; it was about establishing a healthier balance of power in her relationships.

About four months after our initial conversation, Megan walked into my office with news.

"I went to family dinner last night," she said.

I raised my eyebrows. "By choice?"

She nodded. "Completely by choice. After three months of no Wednesday dinners, my mom called on Monday and asked—not demanded, but actually asked—if I might want to join them this week. She said she's missed me."

"And you felt ready?"

"I did," Megan confirmed. "But I went in with clear boundaries. I told myself that if at any point I started feeling diminished or attacked, I would simply say, 'I don't find that helpful,' and if necessary, I would leave."

"That's fantastic." I smiled. "How did it go?"

"Weirdly…better?" Megan looked almost surprised. "Mom was still Mom—she made a comment about my haircut—but instead of just absorbing it, I said, 'I actually love my hair this way.' And then she just…moved on. No big drama."

"What do you think changed?" I asked.

Megan thought for a moment. "I think I changed. I went in knowing I could leave at any time. That this was my choice, not my obligation. And somehow, that changed how I responded to everything."

"You plugged the power leak," I said. "When you stopped giving your mother the power to define your worth, you changed the entire dynamic between you."

"The strangest part," Megan continued, "is that I think I actually enjoyed parts of the evening. When I wasn't sitting there braced for the next hit, I could appreciate the good things: the food, my niece's stories about school, even some moments with my mom."

"That makes perfect sense." I nodded. "When we're not leaking power, we have more energy to be present and engaged. We can enjoy connections without being depleted by them."

"I'm not saying everything's fixed," Megan cautioned. "Mom is still Mom. These patterns are decades old. But something fundamental has shifted in how I approach the relationship."

"And that shift is…?" I prompted.

"I'm not responsible for her feelings, and she's not in charge of mine," Megan said firmly. "I get to decide what I will and won't accept in our relationship. I get to hold my power instead of giving it away."

THE PRACTICE

Megan's expedition illustrates the three essential steps to plugging power leaks in any relationship:

1. RECOGNIZE WHERE YOU'RE GIVING YOUR POWER AWAY.

For Megan, this meant seeing how she had accepted responsibility for her mother's emotions and how that had led to prioritizing family harmony over her own well-being and participating in a dynamic that consistently diminished her.

To identify your own power leaks, ask yourself:

- In what situations do I feel resentful, exhausted, or smaller afterward?
- When do I say "yes" when I really want to say "no"?
- Whose emotions or reactions do I feel responsible for managing?
- Where do I silence or diminish myself to make others comfortable?

- What parts of myself do I hide or change depending on who I'm with?

Each of these questions points to places where your power might be leaking out.

2. CREATE BOUNDARIES THAT PROTECT YOUR POWER.

Megan's boundary was initially quite broad—she needed to completely step away from the weekly dinners to reclaim her sense of self. Later, as she grew stronger in her power, she was able to create more nuanced boundaries about how she would engage with her family.

Boundaries aren't about controlling others; they're about clarifying what you will and won't accept, what you will and won't do.

Effective boundaries:

- focus on your actions, not others' behavior
- are stated clearly and directly
- include outcomes you're willing to enforce
- evolve as you and your relationships change

When Megan returned to the family dinner, her boundary wasn't "My mother can't criticize me" (which would be trying to control someone else's behavior). Instead, it was "If I start feeling diminished, I will speak up and, if necessary, leave" (which focuses on her own actions and responses).

3. HOLD YOUR BOUNDARY WITH COMPASSIONATE FIRMNESS.

This is often the hardest part. When others push back against our boundaries—with guilt, anger, manipulation, or even genuine hurt— our instinct is often to concede in order to restore harmony.

Megan faced significant pushback from both her mother and sister. She weathered this storm by:

- reminding herself that their reactions belonged to them, not her
- consistently restating her need for space without defensiveness or apology
- accepting that some people would be upset with her choices
- staying connected to her deeper values of self-respect and authenticity

Holding boundaries doesn't mean being rigid or uncaring. We can acknowledge others' feelings without taking responsibility for them. We can express love while still maintaining our limits. We can be open to negotiation without abandoning our core needs. This is our part of the dance.

As Megan discovered, when we hold our boundaries consistently over time, something remarkable often happens: The relationship itself begins to transform. People who are used to us leaking power will initially push hard against our new limits. But if we stay firm, most people eventually adjust to the new reality, and some relationships even become healthier as a result.

The fundamental truth about power leaks is this: Your power belongs to you. Not to your parent, not to your partner, not to your boss, not to your children, not to society's expectations—to you.

You get to decide how you use your power. You get to determine what you will and will not accept. You get to affirm your own worth rather than outsourcing that job to others.

This does not mean disconnecting from relationships or responsibilities. It means showing up to those relationships as a whole person with clear boundaries, rather than as a hollow shell whose primary purpose is to fulfill others' needs and expectations.

When Megan first came to see me, she believed she had only two options: continue attending those painful weekly dinners or completely cut off her family. What she discovered was a third option, one where she could stay connected to her family while also staying connected to herself.

That's the gift of plugging your power leaks. You don't have to choose between self and other, between authenticity and relationship. When you hold your power with confidence and compassion, you create the possibility for connections that are both genuine and sustainable.

CHAPTER 9

FINDING YOUR STYLE

OUR RELATIONAL STYLE is our unique way of how we express ourselves. When our style interacts with someone else's style, it makes a beautiful dance that we call a pattern of the relationship. Sometimes, our style gets hijacked. We get confused or shut down by what seems like an unexplained but recurring emotion. Tracking this emotion can lead us to answers that can free our style to be what it is really designed to be.

"It happened again," Sophia said, her voice tight with frustration. "I completely shut down in that meeting. My boss asked for input on the new project, and even though I had ideas—good ones—I couldn't get the words out. Everyone else was speaking up, and I just sat there, silent. Then I spent the rest of the day beating myself up about it."

Sophia was a brilliant marketing strategist in her early thirties. She had an impressive resume, a sharp mind, and insights that often changed the direction of projects for the better. She knew her gifts, and she usually had a warm style of expressing herself with them. But she had a recurring emotion that was holding her back professionally:

In certain meetings, particularly with senior leadership, she would feel anxious, freeze up, and go silent, unable to voice her thoughts.

"This has been happening for as long as I can remember," she continued. "In school, in my first job, and now here. I know I have valuable things to contribute, but in those moments, it's like my brain just…shuts off."

"What are you feeling in those moments when you freeze?" I asked.

"Anxious. My heart races. My throat gets tight. I feel like everyone's staring at me, waiting for me to say something stupid."

"And what goes through your mind?"

"That I'm going to sound foolish. That they'll realize I don't belong there. That I've somehow fooled everyone into thinking I'm competent, but if I speak up, they'll see the truth."

I nodded. "Classic impostor syndrome. But I'm curious about something. Are there any situations where you don't experience this freeze response? Are there time when you do feel comfortable speaking up?"

She thought for a moment. "With my team—the people who report to me—I'm fine. I can express my thoughts clearly, debate points, even push back when needed. It's just when I'm with people more senior than me, especially in formal settings, that I lock up."

"What's different about those situations?"

"I guess…with my team, I know I'm the expert. They look to me for direction. But with senior leadership, I feel like I'm being evaluated. Like I need to prove I deserve to be in the room."

Recognizing and understanding our recurring emotion means understanding these aren't just isolated reactions, but themes that play out across different situations and relationships throughout our lives.

Sophia's recurring emotion was clear: In situations where she felt evaluated by authority figures, she experienced anxiety, self-doubt, and a freeze response that prevented her from expressing her ideas. This was a consistent pattern that had been playing out since her school days.

Understanding these patterns—not just what triggers them, but why—is essential for developing true self-awareness and creating the possibility for change. These patterns are like emotional templates or scripts that get activated in certain types of situations. They include:

- the events that set off the pattern
- the emotions that arise as a result of the event
- how we interpret this event
- the behaviors that follow and their impact on the environment
- the impact this event has on our sense of self and how we see others

For Sophia, the pattern looked like this:

Event: Being in meetings with senior leadership; being asked to contribute on the spot; formal evaluation contexts

Emotions: Anxiety, fear, self-doubt

Interpretations: "I'll sound stupid"; "They'll realize I don't belong"; "I'm a fraud"

Behaviors: Freezing up; remaining silent; avoiding eye contact

Impact: Missing opportunities to contribute; reinforcing self-doubt; creating distance from colleagues; limiting career advancement

Once we recognize these patterns, we can begin to understand what activates our recurring emotion—the deeper meanings, past experiences, and core narrative behind it.

THE CORE NARRATIVE

Our emotional patterns develop as adaptive responses to our early experiences or environment. What may have been a helpful or protective response in one context becomes a habitual reaction that continues long after it's useful.

As Sophia and I explored her pattern more deeply, its origins began to emerge. She recalled a formative experience from sixth grade:

"I had this math teacher, Mr. Davis. He would call on students randomly to solve problems at the board. One day, he called on me for a particularly difficult problem. I went up, confident I knew the answer, but I made a simple calculation error. He didn't just correct me—he humiliated me in front of the class. 'This is what happens when you think too highly of yourself,' he said. 'Maybe this will teach you some humility.'"

She continued, "He had made comments like this throughout the year. But after that day, I became terrified of being called on. I would know the answer but wouldn't raise my hand. Eventually, I convinced myself I wasn't really good at math, even though I'd always excelled at it before."

This early experience—being humiliated by an authority figure for making a mistake—created a template that continued to shape Sophia's emotional reactions decades later. What began as a response to a specific situation became generalized to any context that shared similar elements: authority figures, public evaluation, the possibility of making a mistake.

This is how emotional patterns form. An experience creates a powerful learning imprint, and our minds generalize from that experience to protect us from similar harm in the future. The problem is that this generalization often becomes overly broad, activating in situations that merely resemble the original context but do not pose a similar threat.

Understanding the origin does not magically dissolve the pattern, but it does begin to loosen its grip. When we can see our reactions not just as automatic responses to current triggers but as adaptations to past experiences, we gain perspective and learn there is a potentially different choice.

QUESTIONS TO ASK YOURSELF

To uncover and understand your emotional patterns, you need to ask deeper questions than simply "What am I feeling?" or "What triggered me?" Here are the questions that can help reveal the patterns and their origins:

1. WHAT FEELS THREATENING ABOUT THIS SITUATION?

This question helps you identify what aspect of the trigger is activating your emotional response. Is it the possibility of rejection? The fear of looking foolish? The sense of not having control?

For Sophia, what felt threatening about speaking in meetings with senior leadership was the possibility of evaluation and judgment—of being exposed as "not good enough" in front of people whose opinion mattered to her professionally.

2. WHERE HAVE I FELT THIS BEFORE?

This question connects your current reaction to past experiences with similar emotional flavors. The situations might look different on the surface, but the emotional resonance is the same.

When Sophia reflected on this question, she realized that her reaction in meetings had the same emotional quality as her experience with Mr. Davis—the same tightness in her throat, racing heart, and sense of being exposed to potential humiliation.

3. WHAT AM I AFRAID THIS MEANS ABOUT ME?

This question reveals the core beliefs or fears underlying the pattern. What meaning are you giving to the situation that makes it so threatening?

For Sophia, her fear was that being wrong or making a mistake would reveal her as fundamentally inadequate—that she didn't really belong in her role and had somehow fooled everyone into thinking she was competent.

4. How did I learn to respond this way?

This question explores how your pattern developed as an adaptation or protective strategy. How did this response help you cope with past situations?

Sophia's freeze response had originally developed as protection against further humiliation. By not speaking up, she couldn't be wrong or criticized. What began as a strategy to avoid a specific teacher's ridicule became her default response to any situation that felt evaluative.

5. How is this pattern affecting my life now?

This question examines the current impact of the pattern on your relationships, work, and well-being. Is this pattern still serving you, or is it creating limitations?

Sophia's pattern was clearly limiting her professionally. Her inability to speak up in key meetings meant her ideas weren't being heard, she wasn't getting credit for her insights, and she was being passed over for opportunities that required visible leadership.

6. Where can I experiment with a new response?

Once you can recognize the pattern as it's happening, experiment with small shifts in your response. This isn't about forcing yourself to react differently, but about creating space for choice where there was previously only automatic reaction.

For Sophia, this meant preparing one point to share in each meeting, taking deep breaths when she noticed anxiety arising, and reminding herself, "This feeling is familiar—it's my old pattern from Mr. Davis, not a reflection of the current reality."

"I still get nervous," she told me in a later session, "but now I understand why. And that understanding itself somehow makes the anxiety less overwhelming. I can see it as an old pattern rather than a reflection of reality."

"Last week, we had a big strategy meeting with the C-suite. I felt that familiar tightness in my throat when the CEO asked for input. But instead of getting swept away by it, I thought, There's my Mr. Davis pattern. I had prepared one point I wanted to make, so I took a deep breath and focused just on saying that one thing."

"What happened?" I asked.

"I got it out," she said with a smile. "It wasn't eloquent, and my voice shook a bit, but I said my piece. And you know what? The CFO actually built on my point and said it was an important perspective. Nothing terrible happened. I didn't get humiliated or exposed as a fraud."

This was significant progress. Sophia didn't eliminate her anxiety, but she had created space between the trigger and her response. She was no longer completely identified with her pattern; she could see it as an old adaptation rather than a necessary reaction to the present moment.

As our work continued, Sophia had even more insight:

"I realized something this week. This pattern doesn't just show up at work—it's affected my personal relationships too. When my partner criticizes me, even gently, I have the same reaction: I freeze up, can't find words, then beat myself up later for not expressing what I really wanted to say." This recognition of how her pattern played out across different domains of her life deepened Sophia's understanding and expanded her opportunities for change.

Recognizing our core narrative helps us address patterns at their root rather than just managing individual symptoms. Instead of developing separate strategies for speaking up in meetings, applying for promotions, and accepting compliments, Sophia could work with the underlying beliefs that connected all these situations.

Over time, our emotional patterns become interwoven with our sense of who we are. We start to define ourselves by our patterns: "I'm just shy" or "I have a temper" or "I'm a perfectionist." We mistake these ways of expressing ourselves as our true styles. They are not.

This identification makes these shifts in our styles particularly difficult to change. It's one thing to modify a behavior; it's another to contemplate changing something that feels like an intrinsic part of your identity.

Part of Sophia's path involved recognizing how her pattern had become entangled with her self-concept. She had defined herself as "someone who's better behind the scenes" and "not a public speaker," styles that both reflected and reinforced her pattern.

As she worked with her pattern, she began to question these self-definitions. Was she really "not a public speaker," or was that just a story she'd created to accommodate her anxiety? What parts of her identity were authentic expressions of her true self, and what parts were adaptations to old wounds and fears?

This questioning opened up new possibilities for who she was and how she could express herself—not by forcing herself to become someone new, but by releasing the constraints of identities built around protective patterns. She was able to find her true style!

"I just don't get it," Vanessa said, leaning forward in her chair. "How do I keep ending up here?"

It was our third session together. Vanessa, a bright, accomplished woman in her mid-thirties, had sought therapy after ending her fourth significant relationship in seven years—each one following a similar, painful trajectory.

"Tell me about 'here,'" I encouraged. "What does 'here' look like to you?"

She sighed. "It looks like me, once again, feeling responsible for someone else's emotional state. It looks like me exhausting myself trying to fix someone who doesn't want to be fixed. It looks like me losing myself completely, then waking up one day and wondering where I went."

I nodded. "And this pattern feels familiar from your previous relationships?"

"Painfully familiar," she confirmed. "The details change, but the story is the same. I meet someone with potential but problems. I convince myself I can help them reach that potential. I pour everything into 'supporting' them while ignoring red flags. Eventually, I'm drained dry, resentful, and wondering how I missed all the warning signs that were there from day one."

"That's a remarkably clear description of your pattern," I observed. "What do you think keeps pulling you back into this story?"

Vanessa was quiet for a moment. "I guess I'd like to believe it's just bad luck. Wrong place, wrong time, wrong person. Four times in a row." She gave a humorless laugh.

"But you don't quite believe that," I suggested.

"No," she admitted. "I'm starting to think I might be the common denominator here."

"That's a powerful insight," I acknowledged. "If you are the common denominator—and I think there's wisdom in considering that possibility—what might be happening inside you that creates this recurring pattern?"

Vanessa looked out the window, considering. "I've always been the responsible one, the fixer, the person everyone counts on. My mom relied on me emotionally after my dad left. My younger brothers needed me to step up. I was the one who held everything together."

"So taking care of others became part of your identity," I suggested.

"More than part of it," Vanessa corrected. "Sometimes, I think it's the whole thing. If I'm not taking care of someone, who am I?"

That question—"Who am I?"—would become the foundation of our work together. Because underneath Vanessa's relationship style was a more fundamental issue: She had learned to define herself through her relationship to others rather than through a solid sense of her own identity and worth.

We all have relationship styles, habitual ways of engaging with others that have become so automatic we barely notice them. These styles aren't random. They're shaped by our earliest experiences of connection, the roles we learned in our families of origin, and the strategies we developed to feel safe and valued in our formative relationships.

Our relationship styles include:

- the roles we automatically assume (caretaker, peacemaker, advisor, entertainer)
- how we respond to conflict (avoid, accommodate, control, problem-solve)
- the kinds of behaviors we're drawn to or repelled by in others
- how much of ourselves we reveal or conceal
- where we tend to lose our boundaries or sense of self
- what beliefs we hold about what we deserve or can expect from relationships

The problem with our styles is that we might have unknowingly interwoven them without a core narrative. We move through our relationships on autopilot, unconsciously recreating familiar dynamics, then wonder why we keep ending up in the same painful scenarios with different people.

Exploring your relationship style is the first step toward making more conscious choices about how you show up with others. It's about recognizing your default settings and understanding where they came from, so you can decide which style serves your authentic self.

"I'd like to go back to something you mentioned earlier," I said to Vanessa in our fourth session. "You talked about becoming 'the responsible one' in your family after your father left. How old were you then?"

"Eleven," she replied. "My brothers were seven and five."

"That's young to take on so much responsibility," I observed.

"I didn't really have a choice," Vanessa said. "My mom was barely functioning. Someone had to make sure the boys ate dinner and got to school on time."

"You stepped into a caretaking role out of necessity." I nodded. "And that role became valuable to your family system."

"My mom used to call me her 'little rock,'" Vanessa recalled. "She'd say she couldn't have made it without me."

"That's a lot of weight for a child to carry," I said gently. "Being someone's rock."

Vanessa's eyes filled with tears. "But I was good at it. It was the one thing I knew I could do well: take care of people who were falling apart."

"And that strategy—being the capable caretaker for struggling people—worked in your family system," I noted. "It made you valuable. It gave you a clear role and purpose. It makes sense that you'd carry that strategy forward into your adult relationships."

Vanessa wiped her eyes. "So you're saying I keep choosing partners who need taking care of because that's what I know how to do?"

"I'm suggesting it's a possibility worth exploring," I replied. "When we develop strategies that work in our early environments, we tend to recreate situations where those same strategies are relevant. Not because we want to suffer, but because operating in familiar patterns gives us a sense of competence and identity."

Our most persistent relationship styles usually begin as adaptive strategies in our early environments. They're not random or self-destructive choices; they're solutions to problems we faced in formative relationships.

Ron was another client whose relationship style clearly tracked back to his childhood experiences. As the youngest child in a chaotic, unpredictable family, he learned that humor could defuse tension and draw positive attention. Being funny became his superpower, his way of creating safety and connection.

In his adult relationships, Ron automatically fell into the role of entertainer and tension-breaker. This style had benefits—people enjoyed his company and he was often the life of the party. But it also created problems. He struggled with genuine intimacy because he'd shift to humor whenever conversations got too deep or emotionally charged. His partners complained that they never felt they knew the "real Ron" behind the jokes and stories.

"The thing is," Ron told me, "being funny works. It's gotten me through some really tough situations. People like me when I make them laugh."

"It absolutely works," I agreed. "That strategy has served you well in many ways. The question isn't whether it's effective; it's whether it's sufficient. Does it allow for the full range of connection you want in your close relationships?"

Like Vanessa's caretaking, Ron's use of humor wasn't inherently problematic. The issue was that it had become his only strategy for engagement, his automatic response regardless of the situation or relationship. He had a hammer, so everything looked like a nail.

This is the nature of our earliest relationship style: It's so deeply ingrained that we apply it universally, often without realizing we're doing so. We don't consciously think, *I'll use my caretaking strategy now* or *this is a good time for my humor approach.* We just react according to our established style, then wonder why we keep experiencing the same relationship patterns over and over again. Our styles are made to be more flexible than that.

THE CORE NARRATIVE BENEATH THE STYLE

As Vanessa continued to explore the influence of her emotional pattern and her past experiences on her style, she had an insight:

"I'm noticing something strange," she told me after we'd been working together for about six months. "In almost all of my significant relationships, there's this unspoken agreement that I'll be the strong, capable one, and they'll be the one who needs help. Even with friends who are objectively successful and together, we fall into this relationship pattern where I'm the advisor and supporter."

"That's an important observation," I noted. "What do you think that pattern is about for you?"

Vanessa was quiet for a moment. "I think… I think I'm afraid that if I'm not needed, I won't be wanted."

"Say more about that," I encouraged.

"If I'm not fixing someone or taking care of them in some way, what value do I bring?" she continued. "My worth has always been tied to what I can do for others, not who I am. Being needed feels safe. Being wanted just for myself feels…terrifying, actually."

"Because?" I prompted gently.

"Because what if who I am isn't enough?" Vanessa's voice caught. "What if, without all the fixing and caretaking, there's nothing special about me worth loving?"

"There it is," I said softly. "The core narrative beneath the style."

For most of us, there's a core narrative that drives our relationship style and forms our relationship patterns. This is often a deeply held conviction about our fundamental worth or safety in relation to others.

Some common core narratives that drive relationship styles include:

- "I'm only valuable when I'm useful to others."
- "If I don't keep people happy, they'll leave me."
- "I must be perfect to be lovable."
- "People will hurt or control me if I let them get too close."
- "My needs are less important than others' needs."
- "I can't trust others to be there for me."
- "I must earn love through achievement or caretaking."
- "I'm fundamentally flawed/damaged/unworthy of love."

These beliefs develop early, often pre-verbally, from our experiences in formative relationships. They become the invisible operating system running in the background of our connections, governing how we show up, what we expect, and what we believe is possible in relationships.

For Vanessa, the core narrative driving her style and her relationship patterns was "I'm only valuable when I'm needed." This belief made perfect sense given her childhood experience. When her father left and her mother fell apart, her caretaking became essential to her family's functioning. She received praise and recognition for being the "little rock," the responsible one who held everything together. Her worth became tied to her usefulness in crisis.

This core narrative led Vanessa to unconsciously seek out relationships where she could be needed, to form a style that emphasized her caretaking abilities, and to feel anxious in connections where she wasn't actively fixing or supporting someone. It wasn't that she consciously wanted difficult relationships—it was that relationships with struggling people allowed her to operate from her familiar style for securing love and worth.

"So what do I do with this insight?" Vanessa asked. "Now that I can see my style more clearly?"

"That's the perfect question," I replied. "Awareness is the first step, but it's not the whole path. Now that you can see how you habitually show up in relationships and the core narrative driving that style, you have the opportunity to make different choices."

"It feels overwhelming," she admitted. "Like I'd have to completely reinvent myself and how I connect with others."

"It doesn't have to happen all at once," I reassured her. "Change in a relationship style usually happens gradually, through small, consistent shifts in how you show up."

"What kinds of shifts?" Vanessa asked.

"We might start by experimenting with shifts in your style in existing relationships where you feel safe," I suggested. "What would it look like to show a bit more vulnerability with your friend Donna? Or to step back slightly from the caretaking role with your mother?"

Vanessa nodded thoughtfully. "I can see that. Small changes, not a complete overhaul."

"Exactly," I agreed. "And as you make these shifts, you'll be gathering new evidence about what's possible in relationships—evidence that might begin to challenge that core narrative about only being valuable when you're needed."

Changing an entrenched relationship style requires both insight and practice. Understanding the origins of your style is powerful, but it's through new experiences that lasting change occurs. Small shifts can lead to big changes.

1. PRACTICE GRADUATED VULNERABILITY.

If you typically keep others at arm's length emotionally, experiment with small acts of authentic sharing in safe relationships. This doesn't mean immediately revealing your deepest wounds, but gradually allowing trusted others to see more of your genuine thoughts and feelings.

For Vanessa, this meant occasionally sharing her own struggles with friends who were used to her being the perpetually strong supporter. She discovered that most of her friends welcomed this vulnerability and were eager to reciprocate the support she'd always given them.

2. NOTICE AND INTERRUPT AUTOMATIC ROLES.

When you catch yourself automatically slipping into a familiar role— the fixer, the pleaser, the distancer—pause and ask yourself if this role is serving the current situation and relationship. Sometimes, it will be; often, it won't.

Ron, the entertainer, developed a practice of noticing when he was using humor to avoid emotional intimacy. He wouldn't prohibit himself from being funny, but he'd check in: "Am I using humor now because it's genuinely appropriate, or because I'm feeling vulnerable and want to create distance?"

3. EXPERIMENT WITH NEW BEHAVIORS.

Once you've identified your typical patterns, try deliberate experiments with alternative ways of engaging. If you always accommodate others' preferences, practice stating your own. If you habitually take charge, experiment with following someone else's lead.

One client who identified as a chronic peacemaker set a goal of allowing one disagreement per week to remain unresolved rather than immediately rushing in to smooth things over. She discovered that many conflicts worked themselves out without her intervention, and that some productive tension improved her relationships.

4. SEEK DISCONFIRMING EVIDENCE.

Our core beliefs persist partly because we unconsciously seek evidence that confirms them while dismissing evidence that challenges them. Deliberately look for experiences that contradict your limiting beliefs about relationships.

For Vanessa, this meant noticing instances where she was valued for who she was, not just what she did for others. When a friend expressed delight in simply spending time with her, or her brother called just to chat rather than to seek advice, she would consciously register these experiences as evidence against her "only valuable when needed" belief.

5. BUILD YOUR RELATIONSHIP WITH YOURSELF.

Many problematic relationship patterns stem from a disconnection from our own needs, feelings, and boundaries. Strengthening your relationship with yourself provides a foundation for healthier connections with others.

Vanessa developed a daily practice of checking in with herself about her own emotional state and needs—something she'd rarely done before, having been so focused on others. This simple practice helped her maintain a sense of self even in relationships where she'd previously lost her boundaries.

6. CREATE CONSCIOUS AGREEMENTS.

Many relationship difficulties arise from unspoken expectations and agreements. Practice making these explicit, both with yourself and with others.

One couple I worked with, who had fallen into a parent-child dynamic, created an explicit agreement to notice when they were slipping into these roles and to name it in the moment: "I notice I'm starting to parent you right now" or "I'm acting like a rebellious teenager in this conversation." This awareness alone often helped them shift to a more adult-to-adult interaction.

THE COURAGE TO CHANGE

About a year into our work together, Vanessa met someone new—a relationship that would test her growing awareness of her style.

"He's different from my usual type," she told me. "He's got his life together. He's emotionally mature. He doesn't need me to fix him."

"How does that feel?" I asked.

"Terrifying," she admitted with a nervous laugh. "I keep waiting for the problems to emerge so I can step into my familiar role. But they haven't. And sometimes, I find myself trying to create problems to solve, which is pretty disturbing to recognize."

"That's powerful awareness," I acknowledged. "You're catching the old style as it tries to reassert itself."

"The strangest part is that I'm afraid he'll lose interest because I'm not needed," Vanessa continued. "Even though rationally I know that's not how healthy relationships work, that old core narrative is still so strong."

"What helps when those fears come up?" I asked.

"I remind myself that he's consistently shown interest in me as a person, not just as a helper," she said. "He actually seems to enjoy when I let down my 'I've got everything handled' facade and just be a normal, sometimes-messy human being."

"That sounds like a relationship that might offer you something different," I suggested.

"It is," Vanessa nodded. "But I have to consciously choose it every day. My default is still to fall back into caretaker mode, to look for ways to make myself necessary. Choosing to just be myself, to trust that's enough—it takes real courage."

Changing a long-established relationship style does indeed require courage. When we've operated with a certain style for decades, stepping outside of it feels vulnerable. We're venturing into unknown territory without the protection of our familiar strategy.

This vulnerability is actually a sign that meaningful change is occurring. If altering your relationship style feels comfortable and easy, you're probably not making significant shifts. Real transformation happens at the edge of your comfort zone, where you're stretching into new ways of being without the safety net of established relationship patterns.

The good news is that as you practice new ways of showing up in relationships, what initially feels awkward and frightening gradually becomes more natural. The neural pathways associated with your transformed style strengthen, while those connected to your old style weaken through disuse. You develop a broader repertoire of relationship skills and a more flexible sense of style.

Most importantly, you create the possibility for relationships that reflect and support your authentic self—connections where you can be known and valued for who you truly are, not just for the functions you perform with your style. This is the ultimate reward for the challenging work of finding your style.

CHAPTER 10

FINDING YOUR PREFERENCES

"I'**LL HAVE THE** redfish," Charlotte said, closing her menu decisively.

The waiter nodded and turned to me, taking my order before whisking away our menus. It was date night, and I'd brought my wife to our favorite restaurant, an upscale place downtown with a menu that changed seasonally.

"You always get the redfish," I observed with a smile once the waiter had left.

Charlotte laughed. "I know what I like."

"But have you ever tried the other fish dishes?" I asked, genuinely curious. "They do an amazing halibut, and their salmon is supposed to be exceptional."

"I ordered kangaroo here once," she replied with a slight grimace. "It wasn't good."

I laughed. "Was it too springy?"

She rolled her eyes at my terrible joke, but then grew thoughtful. "I guess I just don't like being disappointed when I go out to eat. The redfish is a sure thing."

"That makes sense." I nodded. "But I wonder if we sometimes miss out on discovering new favorites because we stick with the safe choice."

Charlotte tilted her head, considering this. "Maybe. But how do you know if something new is worth the risk?"

It was a simple question over dinner, but it stayed with me long after our meal. How do we know what we truly prefer versus what we choose out of habit, safety, or inherited expectations? And what do we lose when we default to the "safe" choice rather than exploring our authentic preferences?

We were twenty-eight years into our relationship when I had this conversation with Charlotte about her redfish preference. You might think that after nearly three decades together, we'd know everything there was to know about each other. Yet I'm constantly reminded that self-discovery—and discovering each other—is a lifelong expedition.

This realization was driven home even more powerfully a few months later when Charlotte and I were taking one of our evening walks around the neighborhood. These walks had become a cherished ritual for us, a time to connect and talk without the distractions of screens or household tasks.

"Why do you think you do that?" Charlotte asked me in response to something I'd shared about a recent situation.

I gave her my honest assessment, explaining how I saw the pattern in my behavior and where I thought it originated. She listened attentively, then said something that caught me completely off guard.

"Huh. We've been together for twenty-eight years, and I never realized that about you."

I remember feeling a mixture of surprise and delight. Surprise that there were still significant parts of myself that even my wife—the person closest to me on this planet—didn't fully know, and delight that we were still discovering each other after all this time.

"I'm growing," I told her. "I'm changing. We both are."

This ongoing evolution is part of what makes relationships—and life itself—so rich. But it also raises an important question: How well do we really know ourselves? How many of our "preferences" are actual preferences, and how many are inherited patterns, safety mechanisms, or choices we've never actually examined?

THE UNEXAMINED PREFERENCE

James sat across from me, his frustration evident in the tense set of his shoulders. A successful entrepreneur in his early forties, he'd sought therapy because of conflicts with his teenage son.

"He doesn't respect anything I value," James told me. "I worked my backside off to give him opportunities I never had, and he just threw it back in my face."

"What kinds of opportunities?" I asked.

"I got him into the best private school in the city. I'm paying for elite baseball coaching. I've set up a college fund that would make most parents weep with envy," James listed. "But he's failing classes and talking about quitting baseball to join some garage band."

I nodded. "That sounds really disappointing, especially given the sacrifices you've made."

"Exactly!" James said, clearly feeling understood. "I didn't have any of these advantages growing up. My dad was a postal worker. We lived paycheck to paycheck. I had to fight for everything I got."

"And you want better for your son," I observed.

"Of course," he said. "Isn't that what every parent wants?"

"I'm curious," I said, leaning forward slightly. "If you and I were having this conversation about something else—say, your preference for a particular food or hobby—and I asked you why you liked it, would 'because it's better than what I had growing up' feel like a complete answer?"

James looked confused. "I'm not sure I follow."

"Let me put it another way," I tried again. "You've listed all the things you're providing for your son that you didn't have. But I haven't heard anything about what he wants or values."

"He's sixteen," James said dismissively. "He doesn't know what's good for him."

"Maybe not," I acknowledged. "But I'm wondering if it's possible that you're giving him what you wanted at sixteen, not what he wants now."

James started to object, then stopped, his brow furrowing in thought.

"Let me ask you something else," I continued gently. "If your father had been wealthy enough to send you to an elite private school and pay for specialized sports coaching, would you have been grateful? Or might you have had other dreams that didn't align with his vision for you?"

James was quiet for a long moment. "I would have taken the opportunities," he finally said. "But..." He trailed off.

"But?" I prompted.

"But I might have resented the pressure," he admitted. "My dad never put that kind of pressure on me. He just wanted me to be happy."

"And what do you want for your son?" I asked.

James looked pained. "I want him to be happy too. But I want him to have all the advantages I didn't have."

"What if those two things aren't the same?" I suggested. "What if his path to happiness isn't the path you didn't get to take?"

It was a turning point in our work together—the moment James began to question whether what he thought was best for his son was actually about fulfilling unmet needs from his own childhood. He had inherited a definition of success from his culture and upbringing, never really examining whether it aligned with his own values or his son's.

A common pattern I see in my practice is unexamined preferences. These are the choices we make on autopilot, driven by:

1. **Inherited Values:** "This is what my family/culture says is important."
2. **Reaction Formation:** "I'll do the opposite of what my parents did."
3. **Safety Mechanisms:** "This choice has worked before, so I'll stick with it."
4. **Identity Maintenance:** "This is what someone like me does/wants/values."

These unexamined preferences might seem harmless enough when they involve restaurant orders or entertainment choices. But when they drive major life decisions—career paths, relationship patterns, parenting approaches—they can lead to significant disconnection from ourselves and others.

James was giving his son the life he had wanted as a teenager without stopping to consider whether that aligned with who his son actually was. Similarly, Charlotte was ordering the same fish dish every time without exploring whether her palate had changed or whether she might enjoy something new even more.

In both cases, the unexamined preference provided a type of safety—the comfort of the known, the avoidance of possible disappointment. But it also came with a cost: the missed opportunity to discover something that might bring even greater fulfillment or joy.

EXCAVATING YOUR TRUE PREFERENCES

Lisa came to therapy at a crossroads. At thirty-five, she had achieved significant success in corporate marketing but felt increasingly empty and disconnected from her work.

"I should be happy," she told me during our first session. "I make great money. I have the corner office. I'm respected in my field. But every Sunday night, I get this knot in my stomach thinking about Monday morning."

"What do you think that knot is trying to tell you?" I asked.

Lisa shook her head. "Probably that I'm ungrateful. Do you know how many people would kill for my job?"

"Perhaps," I acknowledged. "But I'm more interested in what you want, not what others might want."

"I don't even know anymore," she admitted. "I've been on this track for so long, I'm not sure I remember why I chose it in the first place."

Over the next few sessions, we began what I call "preference excavation"—a gentle archaeological dig to uncover Lisa's authentic desires beneath the layers of "shoulds" and expectations that had accumulated over time.

"When did you decide to go into marketing?" I asked during one session.

"College, I guess," Lisa replied. "I was good at writing and creative thinking, but my dad said I needed a practical degree. Marketing seemed like a compromise—some creativity but still business-focused."

"And if your dad hadn't weighed in? If you'd been making the decision purely based on what interested you?"

Lisa was quiet for a moment, then said softly, "I would have studied literature. I always loved books—getting lost in stories, understanding different perspectives."

"Tell me more about that love," I encouraged.

As Lisa spoke about her passion for literature, her whole demeanor changed. Her eyes lit up, her gestures became more animated, her voice took on a warmth that had been absent when discussing her marketing career.

"I still read all the time," she told me. "It's my escape. Sometimes, I stay up way too late because I can't put a book down."

"When was the last time you stayed up late working on a marketing project because you couldn't stop?" I asked.

Lisa laughed. "Never."

This was just the beginning of Lisa's path to distinguish her inherited preferences from her authentic ones. Through our work together, she began to recognize patterns of choices that were driven by external expectations rather than internal desires:

- She lived in an upscale neighborhood she didn't particularly enjoy because it was the "right" address for someone at her professional level.
- She spent vacations at beach resorts even though she preferred mountains and forests.
- She maintained friendships with colleagues who shared her career ambitions but not her deeper values.
- She dated men who looked good on paper but with whom she felt no genuine connection.

None of these choices were catastrophic on their own. But together, they had created a life that looked impressive from the outside while feeling hollow from within.

THE PRACTICE

So how do we excavate our true preferences from beneath the layers of conditioning, expectation, and habit? Here are some of the approaches Lisa and I used, which you might find helpful in your own exploration:

1. FOLLOW THE ENERGY.

Our bodies often know our true preferences before our minds do. When Lisa talked about literature, she physically lit up—her posture straightened, her eyes brightened, her voice became more expressive. This physical response was a clue to her authentic desire.

To apply this in your own life, pay attention to:

- When do you feel energized versus drained?
- What topics or activities make you lose track of time?
- When do you find yourself naturally leaning in versus pulling back?
- What puts a spontaneous smile on your face?

These bodily responses can be powerful indicators of your true preferences, especially when they contradict what you think you "should" want.

2. QUESTION THE ORIGIN OF YOUR PREFERENCES.

For each significant choice or preference in your life, ask yourself:

- Where did this preference come from?
- When did I first adopt this preference?
- Whose voice am I hearing when I think about this preference?
- If no one else's opinion mattered, would this still be my choice?

When Lisa examined her preference for beach vacations, she realized it stemmed from social media and colleagues' expectations rather than her own enjoyment. She found beaches boring after a day or two but had never questioned whether this "dream vacation" setting was actually dreamy for her.

3. EXPERIMENT WITH ALTERNATIVES.

One of the most powerful ways to discover your true preferences is simply to try something different and notice your response.

I encouraged Lisa to take a weekend trip to a mountain cabin instead of her usual beach resort for her next vacation. She returned with renewed energy and dozens of photos, talking excitedly about the hiking trails and the evening spent by the fireplace reading. The experience confirmed what her body had been trying to tell her: that her authentic preference had been buried beneath an inherited idea of what constituted a "proper" vacation.

4. LISTEN TO YOUR RESISTANCE.

Often, our strongest resistance arises when we're confronted with a truth we're not ready to acknowledge. When I suggested to Lisa that her marketing career might not be aligned with her authentic desires, her immediate response was to defend it and remind me how many people would envy her position.

This resistance was worth exploring. What was she defending against? As we dug deeper, Lisa realized she was terrified of disappointing her father, who had always taken pride in her corporate success. She was also afraid of financial insecurity, having grown up in a household where money was often tight.

These were valid concerns. But by bringing them into conscious awareness, Lisa could begin to distinguish between choices made from fear versus choices made from authentic desire.

5. DIFFERENTIATE BETWEEN THE WHAT AND THE WHY.

Sometimes, our preference for a particular outcome is authentic, but our reasons for wanting it are inherited or externally driven.

James genuinely wanted his son to receive a good education. That preference itself wasn't the problem. The issue was why he wanted it: to fulfill his own unmet childhood needs rather than to support his son's unique path.

By separating the what from the why, we can often retain our authentic preferences while releasing the inherited motivations that distort them.

THE COURAGE TO PREFER

About six months into our work together, Lisa scheduled an emergency session. She arrived looking both terrified and exhilarated.

"I did something crazy," she announced as soon as she sat down.

"Tell me," I encouraged.

"I turned down a promotion," she said. "A big one. Vice President of Marketing. Six-figure raise."

"That does sound significant," I agreed. "What led to that decision?"

"Everything we've been talking about," Lisa explained. "I realized I was about to climb even higher up a ladder that's leaning against the wrong wall. And not just that—I've given notice. I'm leaving in a month."

"That's a major step," I said. "What are your plans?"

"I'm taking some time off," she said. "I've saved enough to give myself a six-month sabbatical. I'm going to read, travel to places I actually want to see, maybe take some literature courses. I don't know exactly what's next, but I know I need space to figure it out without immediately jumping into another 'should.'"

"How does that feel?" I asked.

Lisa took a deep breath. "Terrifying. Thrilling. Like I'm finally taking the wheel of my own life instead of following someone else's map."

"And how did your father react?" I asked, knowing this had been one of her biggest fears.

Lisa smiled ruefully. "Actually, better than I expected. He was concerned, of course. But when I explained how unhappy I've been, he said something that surprised me. He said, 'I never wanted you to be successful at the expense of being happy.'"

"Sometimes, we underestimate the people we're afraid of disappointing," I observed.

"Maybe." Lisa nodded. "Or maybe I'm finally at a place where I can make this choice regardless of his reaction. I love my dad, but this is my life."

That, I thought, was the real breakthrough—not just identifying her authentic preference, but finding the courage to honor it even in the face of potential disapproval or uncertainty.

It takes tremendous courage to choose our authentic preferences over our inherited ones, especially when those authentic choices diverge from family expectations, cultural norms, or established patterns. We risk disappointing others. We risk being wrong. We risk the unknown.

When Charlotte orders something besides the redfish, she risks disappointment. When James allows his son to explore interests outside the prescribed path of achievement, he risks watching his child make mistakes. When Lisa leaves her successful marketing career to find work better aligned with her authentic self, she risks both financial security and her identity as a high achiever.

These risks are real. But so is the cost of living a life driven by un-examined preferences: the slow erosion of vitality, the growing sense of disconnection, the quiet desperation of not knowing who you really are beneath the layers of conditioning and expectation.

The expedition of identifying your true preferences isn't about re-jecting everything from your upbringing or making radical changes for their own sake. Many of our inherited preferences may align perfectly well with our authentic desires. Charlotte might genuinely prefer the redfish over other options. James might discover that he authentically values education and achievement, even after examining these preferences. Lisa might find elements of her marketing career that truly resonate with her authentic self.

The point isn't what you choose—it's how you choose. Do you make decisions on autopilot, defaulting to the safe or expected option? Or do you choose consciously, with awareness of both your conditioned patterns and your authentic desires?

A meaningful life requires both the curiosity to question our inherited preferences and the courage to honor our authentic ones. It calls us to continuous self-discovery—to approach each choice, big or small, as an opportunity to know ourselves a little better.

CHAPTER 11

FINDING YOUR VALUES

"I DON'T KNOW HOW much longer I can do this," Olivia said, her voice barely audible as she sank into the couch in my office. Dark circles shadowed her eyes, and her normally impeccable appearance showed signs of strain: hair pulled back in a hasty ponytail, minimal makeup, shoulders slumped with exhaustion.

"Tell me what's going on," I said.

"Everything. Nothing." She sighed. "I'm doing all the things I'm supposed to be doing. I'm succeeding by every measurable standard. But I feel like I'm dying inside."

Olivia was a thirty-eight-year-old nonprofit executive, mother of two young children, and by all external measures, thriving. Her organization had doubled its impact under her leadership. Her children were healthy and well-adjusted. Her marriage appeared stable. Yet here she was, fighting back tears in my office.

"What brought you in today?" I asked.

"Last week, I found myself sitting in my car in the parking garage at work, unable to make myself get out," she said. "I just sat there for forty-five minutes, staring at the wall, wondering how I was going to make it through another day of meetings and decisions and people needing pieces of me. I've never experienced anything like that before."

I nodded. "That sounds frightening."

"The worst part is, I don't understand it," Olivia continued. "I've worked hard for this career. I love my kids. I have a good marriage. I volunteer for causes I believe in. I'm doing everything right." Her voice cracked on the last word.

"Everything right according to whom?" I asked gently.

She looked at me, confusion evident in her tired eyes. "What do you mean?"

"I mean, whose definition of 'right' are you using to evaluate your life?"

Olivia went quiet, considering the question. "I don't know," she finally admitted. "I guess I've never really thought about it that way."

"Let's try something different," I suggested. "Instead of thinking about what's right or wrong, what you should or shouldn't be doing, I'd like you to tell me about your energy."

"My energy?"

"Yes. When do you feel energized, alive, fully present? And when do you feel drained, depleted, like you're just going through the motions?"

Olivia's brow furrowed. "I'm not sure I understand."

"Our energy—physical, emotional, mental, spiritual—is one of our most reliable guides," I explained. "Yet it's one we're often taught to ignore in favor of external metrics of success or culturally approved choices. But your body knows. Your spirit knows. They're constantly giving you feedback about what truly nourishes you versus what depletes you."

I pulled out a legal pad and drew a simple line down the middle, creating two columns. At the top of one, I wrote "Energizing." At the top of the other, "Draining."

"For the next week, I'd like you to track your energy. Notice when you feel a sense of aliveness, engagement, or flow—even if it's subtle.

Notice when you feel depleted, resentful, or like you're dragging yourself through an activity. Don't judge either response as good or bad. Just observe."

Olivia looked skeptical but took the pad. "That's it? Just notice what gives me energy and what doesn't?"

"For now, yes." I nodded. "Just notice. We'll work with what you discover next time."

We often think about our lives in terms of responsibilities, achievements, and relationships. We measure success by promotions earned, goals accomplished, or milestones reached. These external markers aren't inherently wrong, they're incomplete. They don't tell us anything about the quality of our lived experience, about whether our choices are creating a life that feels meaningful and nourishing to us.

Energy tracking offers a different metric. Instead of asking "Am I doing this right?" or "Should I be doing more?", it asks "Does this choice bring me life or drain the life from me?" This simple shift in perspective can reveal patterns and insights that have been hidden beneath layers of "should" and "must."

When Olivia returned the following week, she carried the legal pad I'd given her, now filled with notes in her precise handwriting.

"What did you discover?" I asked after she'd settled in.

"It was eye-opening," she said, a new alertness in her expression. "I realized that almost everything that energizes me is squeezed into the margins of my life, while my days are dominated by activities that leave me depleted."

"Tell me more about that," I encouraged.

Olivia looked down at her notes. "The biggest surprise was work. I've always identified as someone who loves her career, but when I tracked it honestly, I realized that about 70% of my job drains me completely—all the administrative tasks, the board politics, the endless meetings about meetings."

"And the other 30%?"

A small smile appeared. "That's when I'm working directly with the communities we serve, or mentoring my younger staff, or developing new program ideas. Those parts light me up. But they're a small fraction of how I spend my time."

"What else did you notice?"

"At home, I feel most energized when I'm fully present with my kids—not rushing through bedtime so I can answer emails, but actually playing with them or reading together. But those moments are rare because I'm usually multitasking or thinking about work."

She turned the page of her notes. "The most draining things are the committees I've joined because I 'should,' the dinner parties with my husband's colleagues that always feel like performances, and—this surprised me—most of my volunteer work."

"That last one caught your attention?"

"Yes." Olivia nodded. "I've always volunteered because it feels like the right thing to do. But when I paid attention, I realized I feel resentful and depleted every time I go to the children's hospital fundraising committee. I'm just going through the motions."

"Any other discoveries that surprised you?"

Olivia hesitated, then said, "I took a bath one night after the kids were in bed. Just a simple bath with a book. It was the most energized I'd felt all week, like I could actually feel myself again beneath all the roles I play. How sad is that? A bath was the highlight of my week."

"It's not sad at all," I said. "It's information. Valuable information."

Energy tracking works because it bypasses our rational mind—the part of us that's heavily conditioned by external expectations and "shoulds"—and tunes into our body's wisdom and our spirit's knowing. It reveals the gap between what we think should fulfill us and what actually does.

For Olivia, this simple exercise illuminated a disconnect between the life she'd carefully constructed and the life that would truly nourish her. She'd been operating from an inherited definition of success: prestigious career, beautiful family, community involvement. But underneath this picture-perfect exterior, her energy was steadily draining away.

This pattern is remarkably common. I've worked with countless clients who've built lives that look impressive from the outside while feeling hollow from within. They fill their calendars with commitments that align with societal expectations rather than personal values. They pursue goals they inherited rather than ones they consciously chose. They say yes to obligations that deplete them while saying no to opportunities that might bring them alive.

The result is what philosopher Henry David Thoreau described as "a life of quiet desperation"—going through the motions of a life that may check all the right boxes but doesn't actually feel like yours.

THE THREE DIMENSIONS OF ENERGY

As Olivia and I continued our work together, we explored her energy patterns along three key dimensions: physical, emotional, and spiritual. Each offered unique insights into where her authentic self was being honored and where it was being suppressed.

PHYSICAL ENERGY

"I'm constantly exhausted," Olivia told me in our third session. "I assumed it was just because I have a demanding job and young kids. But after tracking my energy, I'm noticing something different."

"What's that?" I asked.

"Some activities exhaust me in a way that feels…depleting. Like I'm running on fumes. But others tire me out in a way that feels… satisfying. Like I've used my energy for something worthwhile."

This distinction is crucial. Physical tiredness isn't always a negative signal. Sometimes, it indicates that we've engaged our bodies in a way that aligns with our authentic needs—like after a challenging hike or a day spent in meaningful work.

The key question isn't "Does this make me tired?" but rather "Does this tiredness feel depleting or fulfilling?"

For Olivia, sitting in strategy meetings for hours left her physically exhausted in a way that felt empty and draining. In contrast, spending an afternoon gardening with her children tired her out but left her feeling peaceful and content.

By tracking these different physical responses, Olivia began to distinguish between activities that consumed her energy without replenishing it versus those that created a positive energy cycle—requiring effort but ultimately giving back more than they took.

EMOTIONAL ENERGY

Our emotional energy is equally telling. Certain people, environments, and activities consistently generate positive emotional states like joy, curiosity, compassion, or peace. Others reliably produce anxiety, resentment, boredom, or irritation.

"I noticed something about the fundraising committee that bothers me," Olivia said during one session. "It's not just that the meetings are long or that it takes time away from my family. It's that I feel false there, like I'm playing a role rather than being myself."

"What role do you feel you're playing?" I asked.

"The Perfect Volunteer," she said with a wry smile. "Enthusiastic, selfless, always willing to take on more work. But inside, I'm seething with resentment and counting the minutes until I can leave."

"And how does that gap between your outer presentation and inner experience affect you?"

"It's exhausting," Olivia admitted. "I feel like an impostor. And I think that's what drains me the most—not the actual tasks, but maintaining this facade of someone who wants to be there when I really don't."

This emotional incongruence—saying yes when we mean no, pretending interest when we feel boredom, manufacturing enthusiasm when we feel indifference—is one of the most significant energy drains we can experience. It creates a state of constant internal conflict that exhausts us at the deepest level.

In contrast, emotional congruence—when our outer expression aligns with our inner experience—creates a sense of integrity and authenticity that energizes us even in challenging circumstances.

For Olivia, her most emotionally energizing experiences came when she could be fully honest about what she was thinking and feeling, without filtering or performing. These moments were rare, but when they occurred—usually with her closest friend or while writing in her journal—she felt a deep sense of relief and renewal.

Spiritual Energy

The third dimension, spiritual energy, relates to meaning, purpose, and connection to something larger than ourselves. This doesn't necessarily involve religious belief (though it can). It's about whether our activities and choices feel meaningful and aligned with our deepest values.

"I had an unexpected moment at work this week," Olivia told me about a month into our work together. "I was visiting one of our community programs, talking with a young mother who'd benefited from our services. As she was sharing her story, I felt this wave of… I don't know how to describe it…like rightness. Like I was exactly where I was supposed to be, doing exactly what I was meant to do."

"That sounds powerful," I said.

"It was." She nodded. "And it made me realize how rarely I feel that way now. When I first started in this field, I had that feeling all the time. But as I moved up the ladder into administration, those moments became fewer and further between."

This is the essence of spiritual energy: that sense of purpose, meaning, and rightness that comes when our actions align with our deepest values. It's not about specific beliefs but about whether we're living in a way that feels meaningful according to our own internal compass.

For Olivia, direct service to others aligned with her core values in a way that administrative leadership didn't, despite its greater prestige and compensation. When she connected directly with the people her organization served, she experienced a sense of purpose that energized her at the spiritual level. When she was stuck in boardrooms discussing budgets, that connection to meaning was severed.

Energy tracking begins as an exercise in awareness—simply noticing what energizes versus depletes you. But its real power emerges when you use these insights to make different choices. For Olivia, this meant making some significant changes to realign her life with her authentic energy patterns.

"I've been thinking about what you said about my job," she told me about two months into our work. "About how the parts that energize me are such a small percentage of what I actually do."

"What thoughts have you had about that?" I asked.

"Initially, I thought I should just be more grateful. After all, many people would love to have my position," she said. "But then I realized that's exactly the kind of 'should' thinking that got me here in the first place."

I smiled. "So what would your energy say instead of 'should'?"

"It would say that I'm in the wrong role," Olivia admitted. "I'm good at administration, but it drains me. What energizes me is direct service and program development."

Over the next several months, Olivia initiated a transition within her organization. She spoke honestly with her board about her strengths and preferences, and together, they crafted a new role that leveraged her experience while allowing her to focus more on the aspects of the work that energized her. Her compensation decreased somewhat, but the improvement in her quality of life was dramatic.

"I feel like I'm coming back to life," she told me. "I'm still tired—that's the reality of being a working parent—but it's a different kind of tired. More like satisfaction than depletion."

Olivia also made changes in her personal life. She resigned from the fundraising committee that had been draining her and instead found a volunteer opportunity that involved direct service: reading to children at the hospital rather than planning galas to raise money for it. She carved out more time for the simple activities that renewed her, like baths, gardening, and undistracted time with her children.

"The most surprising change has been in my relationships," she reflected near the end of our work together. "When I stopped performing and started being honest about what I actually want and need, some people disappeared from my life. But the relationships that remained became so much deeper and more genuine."

"That makes sense." I nodded. "When we're authentic, we create space for others to be authentic too. We attract connections based on who we really are rather than who we're pretending to be."

"Exactly," Olivia agreed. "I have fewer friends now, but real ones. My husband and I are having conversations we should have had years ago. Even my relationship with my kids feels more genuine; they're getting a real person for a mother, not a performance of perfect motherhood."

Note: I am showing you the positive outcomes. Please know that the struggle is very real. The success of these exercises take repetition and may not yield immediate results. I want to encourage you to stay the course!

THE PRACTICE

Energy tracking has massive transformative potential. By paying attention to what truly energized Olivia versus what depleted her, she was able to make choices that brought her life into greater alignment with her authentic self.

But energy tracking isn't a one-time exercise; it's an ongoing practice. Our energy patterns change as we grow and evolve. Activities that once energized us might become depleting as we enter new life stages or develop different aspects of ourselves. What felt draining in the past might become enlivening as we gain new skills or perspectives.

Here are some ways to make energy tracking a regular practice:

1. CONDUCT REGULAR ENERGY AUDITS.

Set aside time periodically—perhaps monthly or quarterly—to evaluate your current commitments and activities through the lens of energy. Ask yourself:

- Which activities consistently energize me?
- Which consistently deplete me?
- Where do I feel most authentic and aligned?
- Where do I feel like I'm performing or going through the motions?

This regular check-in creates awareness of shifts in your energy patterns and prevents you from staying in depleting situations out of habit or inertia.

2. PRACTICE MINDFUL TRANSITIONS.

The spaces between activities offer valuable opportunities to track your energy. Before leaving one activity and beginning another, take a moment to notice:

- How do I feel after this meeting/conversation/task? More energized or more depleted?
- What specifically gave me energy or drained it?
- Am I looking forward to what comes next, or am I dreading it?

These transition moments can provide immediate feedback about your energy patterns, helping you make more conscious choices about how you spend your time and attention.

3. HONOR YOUR ENERGY CYCLES.

Most of us have natural rhythms to our energy. We have times of day when we're naturally more focused, creative, or social, and other times when we need rest and quiet. We have seasons of productivity and seasons of renewal.

Rather than fighting these natural cycles, work with them as much as you have the latitude to do so. Schedule your most demanding tasks during your peak energy times. Allow yourself periods of rest and recovery. Recognize that both activity and renewal are essential parts of a healthy energy ecosystem.

4. PRACTICE SAYING NO.

For many of us, the biggest energy drain comes from saying yes to commitments that don't align with our authentic values or priorities. Learning to say no—kindly but firmly—is essential to protecting your energy.

This doesn't mean becoming selfish or refusing all requests. It means being discerning about where you direct your limited energy, saying yes to what truly matters to you and no to what doesn't.

5. CREATE ENERGY RENEWAL PRACTICES.

Identify activities that reliably restore your energy and make them nonnegotiable parts of your routine. These might be as simple as a daily walk, regular time in nature, creative expression, meaningful conversation, or spiritual practices that connect you to something larger than yourself.

The specific practices matter less than their effect: Do they reliably help you return to a state of balance and vitality?

BEYOND PRODUCTIVITY

It's important to clarify that energy tracking isn't primarily about maximizing productivity or efficiency. It's not another tool for squeezing more output from yourself. In fact, it often leads in the opposite direction: toward greater spaciousness, depth, and presence rather than increased activity or achievement.

"I used to think self-care was selfish," Olivia told me during one of our last sessions. "Just another item on my to-do list that I never got to. But now I understand it differently. Taking care of my energy isn't separate from taking care of my family or doing meaningful work. It's the foundation that makes everything else possible."

She continued, "When I'm depleted, I have so little to offer anyone. But when I'm energized—really energized, not just caffeinated and pushing through—I show up completely differently. I'm more creative, more compassionate, more present. That benefits everyone in my life, not just me."

This is the paradox of living by your values: By being more selective about where we direct our energy, we actually have more to give to what truly matters. By saying no to what depletes us, we create space to say a more wholehearted yes to what brings us alive.

And isn't that what we really want? Not just a life that looks good on paper or impresses others, but one that feels good from the inside. A life where our outer choices align with our inner knowing, where we're guided by the wisdom of our own energy rather than the expectations of others.

CHAPTER 12

FINDING YOUR PRIORITIES

"I CAN'T BELIEVE I let it happen again," Marcus said, his voice heavy with frustration as he settled into the familiar chair across from me. A successful architect in his early forties, Marcus had been coming to see me for about six months, working through patterns that kept appearing in his relationships, both personal and professional.

"Remember that big project I mentioned last time? The one where the client kept changing the scope but refusing to adjust the timeline or budget?"

I nodded. We'd discussed this situation extensively in our previous session.

"Well, they did it again," Marcus continued. "Called me on Friday afternoon with 'just a few small changes' that will actually require redoing about thirty percent of the design. And guess what I said?" He didn't wait for my response. "I said, 'I'll see what I can do.' Just like I always do."

"And how did that leave you feeling?" I asked.

"Angry. Resentful. Like a doormat." Marcus ran a hand through his hair. "I spent the entire weekend working instead of attending my nephew's birthday party like I'd promised. My sister still isn't speaking to me."

"What stopped you from saying no to the client?" I asked.

Marcus was quiet for a moment. "I kept thinking about how much we need this contract, about the team members whose salaries depend on this work. I told myself it was just one more weekend, one more compromise. But it's never just one, is it?"

"It rarely is," I agreed. "What would have happened if you had said no?"

Marcus looked startled by the question. "The client might have pulled the project. They might have bad-mouthed our firm to others in the industry. We could have lost future work."

"Those all sound like significant fears," I acknowledged. "And they might have some basis in reality. But I'm curious about something. How many times have you compromised your time, your boundaries, your well-being for this client?"

"Too many to count," Marcus admitted.

"And has it made them respect your boundaries more? Has it led to a healthier working relationship?"

Marcus gave a hollow laugh. "Quite the opposite. Every time I say yes to an unreasonable request, they come back with something even more unreasonable."

"So the strategy isn't working," I observed. "Yet you keep employing it, hoping for a different result."

"When you put it that way, it sounds pretty insane," Marcus said.

"Not insane," I offered gently. "Human. We all have places where our boundaries seem negotiable, even when the evidence tells us they shouldn't be. The question is, what makes some boundaries feel flexible while others feel nonnegotiable?"

Marcus considered this. "I don't know. I guess I've never really thought about it that way."

"Let me put it differently," I suggested. "If this client asked you to falsify safety data on a building design, would you do it?"

"Absolutely not!" Marcus looked genuinely shocked. "That would be unethical and dangerous. I'd never compromise on safety, no matter what the cost."

"So that's a nonnegotiable for you." I nodded. "Something you're unwilling to compromise on, regardless of the consequences. What makes that boundary clear and firm, while the boundary around your time and commitments feels more flexible?"

It was a question that would lead us into one of the most important explorations of our work together—the difference between Marcus's true non-negotiables, rooted in his core values, and the negotiable boundaries he'd been treating as if they were written in stone.

We all have boundaries: lines that define where we end and others begin, what we will and won't accept, how we allow ourselves to be treated. But not all boundaries are created equal. Some are genuinely nonnegotiable, reflecting our deepest values and needs. Others are more flexible, subject to context and relationship. The wisdom lies in knowing the difference.

This distinction isn't always obvious. Many of us confuse rigid rules adopted from others—parents, culture, religion, workplaces—with our genuine non-negotiables. We may also discount or negotiate away boundaries that should be firm, as Marcus had been doing with his time and well-being.

Over the next several sessions, Marcus and I worked to clarify his true non-negotiables versus areas where he could afford to be more flexible. This process revealed something surprising. Some of the boundaries he'd been treating as absolute were inherited rules that didn't align with his authentic values, while areas where he consistently allowed violations were connected to needs that were genuinely essential to his well-being.

INHERITED RULES VS. CORE VALUES

"Let's go back to something you said earlier," I suggested during our next session. "You mentioned missing your nephew's birthday party to work on these client revisions. How did that decision get made?"

Marcus shifted uncomfortably. "There wasn't really a decision. The client needed the work done by Monday, so I just canceled my plans."

"What if you'd had tickets to the Super Bowl that day? Or a medical procedure scheduled?" I asked.

Marcus thought about it. "The Super Bowl? I probably still would have canceled. The medical procedure...that depends how serious it was."

"That's interesting. So some commitments feel more cancellable than others. What makes the difference?"

"I guess it comes down to how important they seem," Marcus said. "A kid's birthday party feels less critical than a major client deadline that affects my whole team."

"Who decides what's 'important'?" I pressed gently.

Marcus was quiet for a moment. "I guess I assumed work always comes first. That's how I was raised. My father never missed a day of work in thirty years, but he missed plenty of my baseball games."

"So the belief that work commitments automatically trump family commitments—that's an inherited rule from your upbringing," I observed.

"I suppose it is," Marcus acknowledged. "I never really questioned it."

"What if we question it now?" I suggested. "Not to say it's wrong, but to examine whether it truly aligns with your own values. What matters most to you, Marcus? Not to your father or your industry or your client—but to you?"

Marcus took a deep breath. "Relationships matter to me. Being someone people can count on. Excellence in my work. Making a positive impact on the built environment."

"Those sound like core values." I nodded. "Now, does automatically prioritizing client demands over family commitments serve those values? Or might it sometimes undermine them?"

"When I missed my nephew's party, I definitely wasn't being someone my sister could count on," Marcus admitted. "And honestly, the rush job I did that weekend wasn't my best work either."

"So in trying to honor what you thought was a nonnegotiable—work comes first—you actually compromised several of your core values," I suggested.

"I never looked at it that way before," Marcus said, his expression thoughtful. "So how do I tell the difference between my real nonnegotiables and these...inherited rules?"

This is a crucial question. How do we distinguish between boundaries that reflect our authentic values and needs versus rules we've adopted without examination? Here are some approaches that helped Marcus make this distinction:

1. Trace the Origin of Your "Shoulds."

Many of our inherited rules come packaged as "shoulds": I should always be available to clients. I should never inconvenience others. I should always put work first. These imperatives often have roots in our family systems, cultural backgrounds, or formative experiences.

For Marcus, the belief that work always takes precedence was directly inherited from his father. When we traced this rule to its source, Marcus could begin to question whether it aligned with his own values and priorities rather than accepting it as an unchangeable truth.

This doesn't mean rejecting all inherited wisdom; some family and cultural values may resonate deeply with who we are. The key is conscious choice rather than automatic adoption.

2. NOTICE YOUR PHYSICAL AND EMOTIONAL RESPONSES.

Our bodies often know our true nonnegotiables before our minds do. Pay attention to physical sensations that arise when a boundary is crossed or when you're considering compromising in a particular area.

For Marcus, canceling family commitments for work had become so automatic that he stopped noticing the emotional toll. But when we explored these situations more deeply, he recognized a pattern of resentment, guilt, and emotional exhaustion that signaled a high priority was being ignored.

In contrast, when he imagined compromising on a design safety issue, his physical response was immediate and clear—tension, nausea, a sense of wrongness that registered in his body before his mind could analyze it. This visceral reaction pointed to a genuine nonnegotiable rooted in his core value of professional integrity.

3. EXAMINE THE CONSEQUENCES OF COMPROMISE.

When we repeatedly compromise in areas that connect to our core values and needs, the consequences are far-reaching. We don't just feel momentary discomfort; we experience a growing sense of alienation from ourselves and others.

As we explored the impact of Marcus's boundary violations around time and family commitments, a clear pattern emerged. His relationships were suffering. His health was deteriorating. His enjoyment of his work—once a source of deep fulfillment—was diminishing. These expanding consequences suggested he wasn't just bending a flexible preference but repeatedly violating a genuine need.

"The more I think about it," Marcus said during one session, "the more I realize that having time to recharge and maintaining my relationships aren't luxuries. They're necessities for me to function well in all areas of my life, including work."

"That sounds like the recognition of a nonnegotiable," I nodded.

THE SPECTRUM OF BOUNDARIES

About a month into our exploration, I introduced Marcus to the concept of a boundary spectrum. "Not every boundary falls into the category of absolutely rigid or completely flexible," I explained. "Most exist somewhere on a continuum according to our priorities."

I drew a simple line on a piece of paper and labeled the left end "Flexible" and the right end "Nonnegotiable."

"Let's place some of your boundaries on this spectrum," I suggested.

We started with examples Marcus had already identified. "Safety and ethical standards in your designs—where does that fall?"

"All the way to the right," Marcus said without hesitation. "Completely nonnegotiable."

"What about your weekend time? Where would you place that?"

Marcus thought for a moment. "It's not all-or-nothing. I can be flexible sometimes for genuine emergencies or especially important deadlines. But it can't be every weekend, and it can't be for routine changes that could have been planned better."

I marked a spot about two-thirds of the way toward "Nonnegotiable."

"That's interesting," I observed. "It's not that you're never willing to work on a weekend. It's that you need certain conditions to be met for that to be acceptable: true urgency, infrequency, respect for your time in the planning process."

"Yes, exactly." Marcus nodded. "I don't mind occasionally going above and beyond. I do mind being taken for granted."

We continued placing various boundaries along the spectrum, from highly flexible (like his willingness to compromise on aesthetic elements of designs to meet client preferences) to completely nonnegotiable (his refusal to cut corners on structural integrity, even when pressured).

This exercise revealed an important pattern: Marcus had been treating many mid-spectrum boundaries as if they were at the "Flexible" extreme, while occasionally becoming rigid about matters that weren't core values for him.

"I think I get confused when I'm under pressure," he reflected. "I lose sight of what's truly nonnegotiable for me versus where I can reasonably bend."

"That's a very common experience," I assured him. "When we're stressed or facing potential conflict, our boundary awareness often gets cloudy. That's why it's so helpful to clarify your nonnegotiables before you're in the heat of a difficult situation."

Understanding the difference between genuine nonnegotiables and flexible boundaries is an essential first step. But the real challenge comes in honoring these distinctions in daily life by forming and keeping boundaries.

For Marcus, this meant developing strategies to protect his newly clarified nonnegotiables while maintaining appropriate flexibility in other areas. Here are some of the approaches that worked for him:

1. CREATE CLEAR STRUCTURES.

For priorities that consistently felt difficult to maintain, Marcus created clear, external structures to reinforce them. He blocked off non-working time in his calendar and made it visible to his team. He established a clear protocol for handling "emergency" client requests by distinguishing genuine urgencies from poor planning.

"The structure gives me something to point to," he explained. "Instead of having to make a fresh decision every time a client calls on Friday afternoon, I can simply refer to our established process. It's less personal and less emotionally charged."

2. PRACTICE CLEAR COMMUNICATION.

Many of us struggle not with knowing our boundaries but with communicating them effectively. Marcus had particular difficulty with this aspect, often defaulting to either passive acceptance or unnecessarily harsh refusals.

We practiced alternative responses that were both clear and respectful:

- "That timeline won't work for us, but here's what we can do…"
- "I understand this is important to you. Here's how we need to adjust the scope/budget to accommodate these changes."
- "I've committed to being with my family this weekend. I can start on this first thing Monday morning."

The key was finding language that honored both his boundaries and the relationship—avoiding both doormat and dictator modes.

3. START WITH LOWER-STAKES SITUATIONS.

Changing long-established boundary patterns can feel overwhelming. To build his boundary muscle, Marcus began with situations that felt less threatening—saying no to minor impositions from friends rather than immediately confronting his most demanding client.

"Each small success gave me more confidence," he told me. "I started to see that the world didn't end when I maintained a boundary. In fact, most people adjusted pretty quickly once they realized I was serious."

This gradual approach allowed him to develop both the skill and the courage to address more challenging boundary violations.

4. CONNECT TO THE DEEPER "WHY."

When tempted to compromise on a nonnegotiable, Marcus learned to reconnect with the core value it protected. Rather than getting caught in the immediate pressure of a situation, he would ask himself, "What matters most to me here? What am I really protecting?"

This perspective shift often clarified his priorities and strengthened his resolve. A request wasn't just about working one more weekend; it was about whether he would honor his commitments to family and his need for restoration. The higher stakes made the boundary easier to maintain.

5. ACCEPT THE CONSEQUENCES.

Perhaps the most challenging aspect of holding nonnegotiables is accepting that they sometimes come with significant consequences. For Marcus, this meant potentially losing clients who wouldn't respect his boundaries, disappointing people who had grown accustomed to his constant availability, and possibly even facing financial implications.

"That's the hardest part," he admitted in one of our later sessions. "Knowing that there might be real costs to maintaining these boundaries. But I'm starting to see that there are also real costs to not maintaining them. They're just more hidden and long-term."

This willingness to accept boundary-related consequences—not eagerly or martyr-ishly, but with clear-eyed awareness—is often what distinguishes a genuine nonnegotiable from a preference. We're willing to pay a significant price, if necessary, to honor what truly matters to us.

About six months after we began our work on nonnegotiables, Marcus came to his session with a different energy. The persistent tension I'd observed in his shoulders had eased. He smiled more readily. Even his posture seemed more open and relaxed.

"Something's shifted," I observed.

"Everything's shifted," he replied. "Remember that client I was always complaining about? The one with the constant last-minute changes?"

I nodded.

"I finally had the conversation with them that we'd been practicing," Marcus said. "I explained our new process for handling change requests, including the adjustments to timeline and budget that would be necessary for major revisions. I was fully prepared for them to pull the project."

"And what happened?" I asked.

Marcus laughed. "They apologized! Said they hadn't realized how their process was impacting our team. We worked out a new system that's actually been working pretty well for the past few weeks."

"That's wonderful," I said. "A much better outcome than you feared."

"But here's the thing," Marcus continued, leaning forward. "Even if they had pulled the project, I think I would have been okay with it. For the first time, I felt clear about my nonnegotiables. I knew I couldn't keep operating the way we had been, regardless of the consequences."

"That's a powerful place to stand," I observed.

"It is. And something else unexpected happened," Marcus added. "Some of my team members have thanked me. Apparently, they've been struggling with the same boundary issues but didn't feel they could speak up. By holding the line, I was protecting them too."

This ripple effect is common when we clarify and honor our nonnegotiables. What feels like a personal boundary often creates space for others to recognize and respect their own limits. Our clarity becomes permission for those around us to find theirs.

Nonnegotiables create more genuine relationships. When we're clear about our boundaries, we show up more authentically in our relationships. We're not harboring hidden resentments or performing versions of ourselves that we can't sustain. This authenticity forms the foundation for more meaningful connection.

"My relationship with my sister has improved too," Marcus told me. "I haven't missed a family commitment since that birthday party. But more than that, I think she senses that I'm more fully present when I am there—not checking my phone constantly or mentally back at the office."

"Being physically present is one thing." I nodded. "Being emotionally and mentally present is another level entirely."

"Exactly. And I couldn't do that when I was constantly violating my own boundaries. I was too resentful, too depleted. Now I can actually enjoy the time I spend with people because I'm choosing to be there, not feeling forced or guilted into it."

THE PRACTICE

Your priorities will be uniquely yours, reflecting your specific values, needs, and life circumstances. There's no universal template for what should be nonnegotiable versus flexible. What matters is the alignment between your boundaries and the priorities of your authentic self.

Here are some questions to help you identify your own nonnegotiables:

1. **What violations leave you feeling not just annoyed, but diminished or invisible?** This emotional intensity often signals a boundary connected to a core need or value.
2. **Where do you consistently feel resentment?** Chronic resentment usually indicates a boundary that's being repeatedly crossed.
3. **What do you find yourself thinking about in terms of absolutes?** Phrases like "I could never…" or "I would always…" often point to areas where you have strong boundary clarity.
4. **What has caused you to end relationships in the past?** The breaking points in previous relationships can reveal your nonnegotiables.

5. **What do you regret compromising?** Past regrets often highlight values or needs that are more essential to your well-being than you realized at the time.

6. **What makes you feel most aligned with your authentic self?** The conditions that allow you to feel most genuinely "you" often point to nonnegotiables that protect your core identity.

Once you've identified your nonnegotiables, the next challenge is protecting them in everyday situations. Here are some common scenarios where boundaries get tested, along with reframing responses to help you maintain clarity and courage:

WHEN A FRIEND OR FAMILY MEMBER ASKS FOR HELP YOU CAN'T REASONABLY GIVE

Instead of automatically saying yes or making excuses, try:

- "I care about you, but I'm not able to take that on right now. Is there a smaller way I could support you?"
- "I can't help with that, but I might be able to help you find someone who can."
- "I wish I could help, but my plate is full right now. I need to honor my existing commitments."
- "That doesn't work for me, but I'd be happy to [offer a specific alternative that respects your boundaries]."

WHEN WORK ENCROACHES ON PERSONAL TIME

Instead of reluctantly giving in or responding with resentment, try:

- "I'm not available outside of work hours, but I'll make this a priority first thing tomorrow morning."

- "I don't check email on weekends, but if it's genuinely urgent, here's how you can reach me in a true emergency."
- "I understand this is important. Let's look at what can be postponed or delegated to make room for this new priority during regular hours."
- "I've committed this time to my family. I'll be back online at [specific time] and can address it then."

When a Loved One Pushes Your Emotional Boundaries

Instead of withdrawing or exploding, try:

- "I need some time to process this. Can we pause and return to this conversation in an hour?"
- "When I am spoken to that way, I feel diminished. I would like us to speak respectfully, even when we disagree."
- "This conversation does not seem to be working right now. I'm going to take a break, and I'd like to try again later when we can both be more calm."
- "I understand this matters to you, and it matters to me too. But how we talk about it is just as important as what we decide."

When You Feel Pressured to Spend Money You Don't Have

Instead of caving to pressure or making excuses, try:

- "That's not in my budget right now, but I'd love to [suggest a free or lower-cost alternative]."
- "I'm being more intentional about my spending these days. I'll have to pass on this one."
- "I've already allocated my discretionary funds for this month. I'll have to join you another time."

- "That sounds fun, but it's not a financial priority for me right now."

WHEN YOU'RE EXPECTED TO TAKE ON EMOTIONAL LABOR FOR OTHERS

Instead of absorbing others' emotions or problems, try:

- "I can see you're going through a lot. What do you think would help you with this situation?"
- "I care about what you're experiencing, but I don't have the capacity to take this on right now."
- "I'm happy to listen, but I want to be clear that I can't solve this for you."
- "It sounds like you might benefit from talking to someone with expertise in this area. Would you like me to help you find resources?"

WHEN CULTURAL OR FAMILY EXPECTATIONS CONFLICT WITH YOUR VALUES

Instead of silently complying or being confrontational, try:

- "I understand this tradition is important to you. I'd like to participate in my own way by [offer an alternative that honors your values]."
- "I've given this a lot of thought, and while I respect our family's traditions, I need to make a different choice that aligns with my values."
- "I know this is the way things have always been done, but I'm going to approach this differently. I hope you can respect that, even if you don't agree."
- "This is important to me, and I've made my decision. I understand if you're disappointed, but I need to honor what feels right for me."

WHEN SOMEONE CROSSES A PHYSICAL BOUNDARY

Instead of enduring discomfort or responding aggressively, try:

- "I need a bit more personal space. Would you mind taking a step back?"
- "I'm not comfortable with that kind of physical contact. Let's [suggest alternative greeting or interaction]."
- "Please don't [specific behavior]. I prefer [alternative]."
- "I know you're being friendly, but I don't enjoy [specific type of touch or proximity]. Thank you for understanding."

The key to these alternative responses is that they're clear without being harsh, respectful without being apologetic, and focused on what you need rather than criticizing the other person. They communicate boundaries without attempting to control others' reactions to those boundaries.

Practice these responses or variations that feel authentic to you. The more you use them, the more natural they'll become—and the more you'll discover that many people can handle your boundaries far better than you might have feared.

Remember that nonnegotiables aren't about being rigid or inflexible in all areas. They're about having clarity on what truly matters to you, what you need to thrive rather than just survive. This clarity allows you to be appropriately flexible in areas that aren't connected to your core values and needs.

As Marcus discovered, when we honor our genuine nonnegotiables while maintaining appropriate flexibility elsewhere, we create the conditions for both authentic self-expression and meaningful connection with others. We show up in our relationships as our true selves, clear about who we are and what matters to us, able to engage with others from a place of integrity rather than compromise.

CHAPTER 13

FINDING YOUR CONFIDENCE

"I THINK WE SHOULD stop," Elaine said abruptly, about thirty minutes into our session.

We'd been working together for nearly four months, making steady progress on what she'd initially described as "career confusion." Elaine was a successful corporate attorney in her late forties who, despite her achievements, felt increasingly hollow about her work. Our sessions had been productive, if somewhat circumscribed—she approached therapy with the same analytical precision she brought to legal cases, carefully controlling the pace and depth of our conversations.

But today was different. We'd ventured into territory that felt more personal, exploring not just what she wanted to do professionally, but who she wanted to be. And now, suddenly, she wanted to stop.

"We still have some time left," I observed. "What's coming up for you right now?"

Elaine straightened the sleeve of her perfectly tailored blazer. "I just realized I have a brief due tomorrow that needs my attention. This career exploration has been useful, but I think I should get back to my actual job." Her tone was polite but definitive.

I nodded, giving her space to feel my acceptance of whatever she chose. "Of course. It's always your decision how to use our time together, and whether to continue at all."

Something in my phrasing seemed to catch her off guard. She looked up sharply. "I didn't say I wanted to end therapy entirely."

"You're right, you didn't," I acknowledged. "I'm noticing, though, that we reached a particular kind of edge today, and then you felt a need to step back. I'm curious about that edge."

Elaine was quiet for a moment, her expression guarded. "I don't know what you mean by 'edge.'"

"Well, we were talking about what truly matters to you, beyond external markers of success," I said. "You mentioned that your father always emphasized achievement and social standing, and then you started to say something about a time in college when you considered a different path. That's when you stopped and said we should end the session."

Elaine looked away, her posture still composed but her eyes revealing a flash of something—vulnerability, perhaps, or irritation.

"I'm not trying to push you somewhere you don't want to go," I assured her. "I just think it's worth noticing what happens when we approach certain areas of self-exploration."

"Fine," she said after a moment. "I felt uncomfortable. The conversation was getting…messy. Unprofessional." She said the last word with distaste.

"Messy in what way?" I asked gently.

"You were asking me to talk about feelings and regrets and roads not taken. That's not why I came here. I need clarity about my career trajectory, not some deep journey into my psyche. I'm not broken, Dr. Long."

"I never suggested you were," I said. "But I wonder if there might be a connection between your current career dissatisfaction and those unexplored paths. Not because you made the wrong choice, but because parts of yourself might have gotten left behind along the way."

Elaine checked her watch, an elegant timepiece that subtly communicated both wealth and restraint. "Our time is almost up anyway," she noted, even though we still had fifteen minutes remaining.

I decided not to press further. "Alright. Before you go, I'd like to suggest something to consider before our next session, if you're open to it."

She gave a small nod, already reaching for her leather portfolio.

"What if the clarity you're seeking about your career can't be found solely by analyzing career options? What if it requires understanding more about who you are beyond your professional identity?"

Elaine paused, her hand on her portfolio. "That seems…inefficient."

I smiled at her characteristic response. "Maybe. Or maybe it's the most direct route to what you're actually looking for."

She didn't reply, but I noticed she hadn't continued gathering her things.

"What scares you about looking more deeply at yourself, Elaine?"

The question hung in the air between us. For a moment, I thought she might simply stand and leave. Instead, she surprised me.

"What if there's nothing there?" she said quietly.

THE DEEPER FEARS BENEATH SELF-DISCOVERY

When Elaine voiced her fear—"What if there's nothing there?"—she was touching on something that many of us experience when faced with genuine self-exploration. But as our work continued, I discovered that this initial fear was just the surface of much deeper concerns.

In my years of practice, I've observed that our resistance to self-discovery often stems from complex, layered fears that go beyond simple anxiety about what we might find. These fears touch on fundamental questions of identity, purpose, connection, and meaning—the very foundations of how we understand ourselves and our place in the world.

Let's explore some of these deeper fears.

THE FEAR OF DISMANTLING THE FALSE SELF

"I've been playing a part for so long, I'm afraid I wouldn't know how to live without the script."

This confession came from Elaine during our third month of work together, after she'd begun the tentative process of looking beyond her professional identity. She'd started painting again, had joined a book club focused on philosophy and spirituality, and had even taken a weekend trip by herself to a small coastal town—all small steps toward reconnecting with neglected aspects of herself.

"Tell me more about the 'part' you feel you've been playing," I encouraged.

"Perfect Elaine," she said with a rueful smile. "The one who graduated top of her class, who never shows weakness, who has the right answer for everything. The one who sacrifices personal needs for professional achievement because that's what successful people do." She paused. "I've been her for so long that I'm not sure who I'd be without her."

This fear—that dismantling our carefully constructed false self might leave us without any sense of identity at all—runs deeper than the fear of emptiness. It recognizes that we've invested decades in building and maintaining a particular self-image, one that may have brought us validation, success, or at least safety. The prospect of letting go of this familiar construction, even if it no longer serves us, can feel like stepping off a cliff without knowing what lies below.

"Perfect Elaine" wasn't just a role she played; it was a complete identity system with its own values, rules, and rewards. It had protected her from the vulnerability of authentic engagement while providing external validation through achievement. Stepping away from this identity, even partially, meant entering unfamiliar territory where the old rules no longer applied.

"The irony," Elaine noted in one session, "is that playing this part has become exhausting. Perfect Elaine is dying inside from the effort of maintaining the performance. But the thought of putting down that role still terrifies me."

"What specifically feels most frightening about it?" I asked.

Elaine thought for a moment. "I think it's that I've defined success so narrowly for so long. If I'm not achieving in the ways I've always measured—winning cases, making partner, earning a certain income—then what would success even look like? How would I know if I'm doing life 'right'?"

This question—how to navigate without our familiar metrics of self-worth—often emerges as we consider dismantling the false self. We've relied on certain external validations for so long that we struggle to imagine any other way of determining our value or direction.

As Elaine began experimenting with alternative ways of being, she discovered something surprising: Beneath the exhaustion of performance lay a hunger for a different kind of experience, one based on presence rather than achievement, connection rather than impression management.

"I went to my book club last night without preparing," she told me in one session. "Normally I'd have read the book twice and researched the author extensively—you know, to be the most knowledgeable person in the room. Instead, I just showed up having read it once, with no prepared insights. And it was…liberating. I actually enjoyed the discussion more because I was discovering what I thought along with everyone else, not performing expertise."

These small experiments helped Elaine begin to trust that something vital and genuine existed beneath her carefully maintained facade—not emptiness, but a more authentic way of engaging with herself and the world.

THE FEAR OF DISCOVERING OUR SHADOW

"There's a part of me that I don't let anyone see—that I barely acknowledge to myself. It's angry, selfish, even cruel sometimes. If that's who I really am underneath everything else, I don't want to know it."

These words came from Andrea, a dedicated nurse and mother of three who initially sought therapy for "work-life balance." As we explored her constantly self-sacrificing approach to both her profession and her family, I began to sense a powerful undercurrent of resentment that Andrea refused to acknowledge.

"You give so much to others," I observed in one session. "I wonder if there's a part of you that sometimes just wants to say 'no' or even 'to hell with all of you—what about me?'"

Andrea recoiled from the suggestion. "I would never think that," she insisted. "I love taking care of people. It's who I am."

This reaction—the immediate, almost visceral rejection of less virtuous aspects of ourselves—often signals the presence of what Carl Jung called the "shadow," those parts of our psyche that don't align with our conscious self-image and are therefore relegated to unconsciousness.

For Andrea, whose identity was built around being endlessly giving and patient, acknowledging the existence of anger, resentment, or selfish desires felt profoundly threatening. If she was secretly angry or resentful, what kind of person did that make her?

The fear of discovering our shadow often manifests as rigid adherence to a particular self-image, usually one that embodies qualities we consider virtuous or acceptable. We define ourselves as "the helpful one," "the responsible one," "the peaceful one," or "the strong one," then ruthlessly suppress any feelings or desires that contradict this definition.

The irony is that these disowned aspects don't disappear; they operate from the shadows, emerging in indirect ways through passive-aggressive behavior, psychosomatic symptoms, dreams, or projections onto others. Andrea's unacknowledged anger wasn't absent from her life. It showed up in mysterious migraines, in her hypercritical thoughts about "selfish" colleagues, and in the emotional distance she maintained in intimate relationships.

"I had the strangest dream last night," Andrea told me several months into our work. "I was at the hospital, and a patient kept pressing the call button repeatedly for minor things. In real life, I would just keep responding patiently. But in the dream, I walked in and yanked the call button out of the wall. Then I looked at the patient and said, 'Figure it out yourself for once.' And the weird thing is, I woke up feeling…relieved."

"That dream gave voice to a part of you that doesn't get much expression in your waking life," I suggested.

"The angry part," Andrea said quietly.

"The part that has limits and needs and doesn't want to be endlessly available to others," I offered. "The part that knows that sometimes saying 'no' to others means saying 'yes' to yourself."

Over time, Andrea began to cautiously acknowledge and explore her shadow—not just her anger and resentment, but also her desires, her ambitions, and her need for solitude. Far from confirming her fear that she was secretly a terrible person, this exploration revealed that her shadow contained not only difficult emotions but also strengths she'd been denying: healthy assertiveness, clear boundaries, and a legitimate need for self-care.

"I was so afraid that if I acknowledged my anger, I'd become this awful, selfish person," Andrea reflected toward the end of our work together. "But actually, the opposite happened. When I stopped pretending those feelings didn't exist, they became less intense and overwhelming. I can feel angry without being consumed by it. I can set boundaries without guilt. I'm a better nurse and mother now because I'm not constantly running from parts of myself."

This transformation—from fearing our shadow to integrating it as a source of wholeness and authenticity—represents one of the most significant shifts that can occur through the process of self-discovery.

THE FEAR OF FINDING NO DEEPER PURPOSE

"What if I look inside and discover there's nothing I truly care about? What if all my achievements have just been about proving myself, and there's no real meaning behind any of it?"

This question came from Richard, a successful entrepreneur in his early fifties who had recently sold his technology company for a substantial sum. What should have been a triumphant moment instead precipitated an existential crisis that brought him to my office.

"I've spent thirty years climbing a ladder," Richard told me. "Building businesses, making money, expanding my influence. I was so busy climbing that I never stopped to ask if the ladder was leaning against the right wall. Now I'm at the top, and I feel…nothing."

Richard's fear touched on something many high achievers eventually confront: the possibility that their drive has been fueled primarily by external validation or the need to prove their worth, rather than by authentic purpose or meaning. The prospect of discovering this void can be terrifying, especially for those who have invested decades in achievement-oriented pursuits.

"I'm afraid to really examine my motivations," Richard admitted. "What if I discover that nothing actually matters to me? That I've just been running on the hamster wheel of success without any deeper purpose?"

This fear—that self-discovery might reveal a fundamental meaninglessness or lack of authentic purpose—often emerges at transition points when external markers of success no longer provide the satisfaction they once did. Retirement, the sale of a business, children leaving home, or reaching long-sought career goals can all trigger this existential questioning.

For Richard, the expedition toward finding authentic purpose involved several distinct phases. First came the painful recognition that much of his drive had indeed been about proving his worth—specifically, overcoming a childhood narrative that he would never amount to anything. This recognition was initially devastating, seeming to confirm his fear that his achievements were hollow.

But as our work continued, Richard began to identify threads of genuine meaning that had been present throughout his career, though often overshadowed by his need for validation. His commitment to mentoring younger employees. His interest in leveraging technology to solve meaningful problems. His concern for creating a workplace culture where people could thrive.

"These values were always there," Richard realized. "But they were secondary to my drive for success. What if I built the next chapter of my life around these deeper values instead of just achievement for its own sake?"

This shift—from fear of meaninglessness to curiosity about authentic purpose—opened new possibilities for Richard. Rather than retiring to a life of leisure as he'd originally planned, he began exploring ways to mentor young entrepreneurs from disadvantaged backgrounds, combining his business expertise with a newfound commitment to creating opportunity for others.

"I still worry sometimes that I'm fooling myself—that I'm just trying to feel important again," Richard told me toward the end of our work together. "But when I'm sitting with these young people, helping them navigate challenges I've faced, it feels different than chasing success. It feels…quiet, but meaningful. Like I'm finally using my experiences for something beyond just adding to my own pile."

This discovery—that authentic purpose often feels qualitatively different from achievement-driven activity—is common among clients who face this particular fear. The meaning they eventually uncover may not be dramatic or world-changing, but it connects to genuine values and creates a sense of alignment that was missing in their previous, externally validated pursuits.

THE FEAR OF AUTHENTIC CONNECTION

"If people saw who I really am—all of me, not just the polished, competent version I show the world—they wouldn't want anything to do with me."

This belief, expressed by Elaine during one of our later sessions, points to perhaps the most fundamental fear underlying resistance to self-discovery: the fear that our authentic self is fundamentally unworthy of love and connection.

Many of us develop elaborate strategies for earning acceptance: through achievement, caretaking, entertainment, agreeableness, or other forms of performance. We believe, often unconsciously, that these performances are necessary because our authentic self would not be enough to secure the connection we desperately need.

For Elaine, this fear manifested in her relentless drive to be perfect—unfailingly composed, articulate, and in control. The thought of allowing others to see her vulnerability, uncertainty, or need felt threatening.

"I had this moment in the partners' meeting last week," she told me several months into our work. "I was presenting a complex case, and one of the senior partners asked a question I hadn't anticipated. In the past, I would have faked my way through an answer, terrified of admitting I didn't know something. But this time, I just said, 'That's an excellent question, and I don't have a ready answer. Let me look into it and get back to you tomorrow.'"

"How did that feel?" I asked.

"Terrifying. And then…okay. The world didn't end. Nobody seemed to think less of me. The meeting continued, and I actually felt more present for the rest of it because I wasn't busy pretending to know everything."

This small act of authenticity represented a significant challenge to Elaine's core fear: that being anything less than perfect would lead to rejection or abandonment. This transformation—from believing that performance is necessary for connection to discovering that authentic expression actually creates the possibility for connection—represents one of the most healing shifts that can occur through self-discovery. It challenges the core belief that our authentic self is unworthy of love, replacing it with the lived experience that genuine connection really only becomes possible precisely as we risk being more fully ourselves.

THE PRACTICE

If you recognize yourself in any of these fears about self-discovery, you're in good company. These concerns are normal, natural responses to the prospect of venturing into deeper self-knowledge. The question isn't whether you'll experience fear, but how you'll relate to it when it arises.

Here are some approaches that have helped my clients move through their fears about self-discovery:

1. NAME THE SPECIFIC FEAR.

Vague anxiety about self-exploration becomes more manageable when we identify exactly what we're afraid might happen. Simply naming the specific fear creates some space around it; we can observe it rather than being completely identified with it. "I notice I'm afraid that looking at my true feelings about my job might force me to make changes I'm not ready for" is a very different stance than being silently gripped by anxiety whenever the topic arises.

2. TRACE THE FEAR TO ITS SOURCE.

Our fears about self-discovery often have roots in early experiences where authenticity was met with negative consequences. Maybe expressing certain emotions wasn't tolerated in your family. Perhaps being "too much" in some way led to rejection or criticism. Or you might have learned that your worth was tied to achievement or appearance rather than authentic being.

Understanding these origins doesn't immediately dissolve the fear, but it helps us recognize that our concerns are based on past conditions that may no longer apply. The consequences we anticipate—rejection, abandonment, invalidation—made sense in our earlier environments but may not be inevitable in our current lives.

3. TAKE SMALL, EXPERIMENTAL STEPS.

Self-discovery doesn't have to be an all-or-nothing plunge into the unknown. We can take measured steps, testing the waters of greater authenticity in contexts that feel relatively safe.

These small experiments serve multiple purposes. They make self-discovery less overwhelming by breaking it into manageable pieces. They provide information about what happens when we express more of our authentic selves (which is often far less catastrophic than we feared). And they gradually build our capacity to tolerate the vulnerability of being more fully seen.

4. CREATE SAFETY FOR THE EXPEDITION.

While self-discovery involves some inevitable discomfort, we can create conditions that support our exploration. This might mean ensuring basic stability in our lives before diving into the deepest questions. It often includes finding companions for the expedition—a therapist, trusted friends, a support group—who can offer perspective and encouragement when fears arise.

This principle extends beyond formal therapeutic relationships. Any context where you feel genuinely seen and accepted can provide a foundation for deeper self-exploration. The key is finding spaces where you don't have to perform or achieve to be valued, where your authentic presence is welcome, including your doubts, fears, and imperfections.

5. REFRAME THE ADVENTURE AS EXPANSION, NOT REPLACEMENT.
Many fears about self-discovery stem from an assumption that what we'll find will somehow negate or invalidate who we've been. But authentic self-discovery is rarely about wholesale replacement of identity. It's more often about expansion: including more of our genuine complexity, recovering parts that have been suppressed, integrating aspects that have been compartmentalized.

This reframing from replacement to expansion can significantly reduce the fear associated with self-discovery. We're not losing who we've been; we're becoming more fully who we are.

THE COURAGE TO KNOW YOURSELF

In a later session, Elaine reflected on the adventure she'd undertaken since that pivotal moment when she'd almost walked out of therapy.

"I was so afraid of what I might find if I looked beyond my professional facade," she said. "I had this image of discovering a vast emptiness—that without my career achievements, I'd be nothing."

"And what have you actually found?" I asked.

She smiled. "Something much more interesting and complex. I've found the parts of myself I set aside decades ago: my creativity, my curiosity about ideas beyond the law, my capacity for wonder. I've found values that were always there but had gotten buried under the pursuit of success. I've even found a kind of strength I didn't know I had—the courage to be more authentic even when it doesn't fit neatly into others' expectations."

"That doesn't sound like emptiness," I observed.

"Not at all," she agreed. "It's actually the opposite, a fullness I'd forgotten was possible."

Elaine's experience exemplifies what I've seen repeatedly in my practice: The fears that initially hold us back from deeper self-knowledge rarely match the reality of what we discover. What looks like a threatening abyss from a distance turns out, upon closer inspection, to be fertile ground for a more authentic and vital way of being.

This doesn't mean the expedition is without challenges. Genuine self-discovery does involve facing uncomfortable truths, questioning long-held assumptions, and sometimes making difficult changes. But these challenges are the price of admission to a more conscious and intentional life, one where our choices emerge from our authentic values and desires rather than unconscious conditioning or external expectations.

The alternative—remaining within the confines of a limited self-concept, avoiding the deeper questions about who we are and what truly matters to us—might seem safer in the moment. But over time, this avoidance exacts its own cost in the form of disconnection, diminished vitality, and the quiet grief of an unlived life.

As you continue your own expedition of self-discovery, I encourage you to notice the fears that arise along the way. Rather than being derailed by them, consider what they might be telling you about your early experiences, your current beliefs about yourself, and the changes that might be possible if you were to move beyond these limitations.

The path to knowing yourself more fully isn't always comfortable, but it is reliably meaningful. And as countless clients have discovered over my years of practice, what waits on the other side of fear isn't the catastrophe we anticipate, but the possibility of a more authentic, connected, and purposeful way of being in the world.

CHAPTER 14

FINDING YOUR SELF-TRUST

"I CAN'T TRUST MYSELF," Veronica said, her voice shaking. "I've been wrong too many times."

I'd been working with Veronica for about three months. A thoughtful woman in her early thirties, she'd initially sought therapy for what she called "chronic indecision" that was affecting both her career and personal relationships. Every choice, from what to order at a restaurant to whether to accept a job offer, became a tortuous exercise in second-guessing and anxiety.

"Tell me about being 'wrong,'" I encouraged. "What does that mean to you?"

Veronica sighed. "I stayed in a relationship for five years with someone who was emotionally unavailable, convincing myself it would get better. I took a job that looked prestigious but made me miserable because I thought I 'should' want it. I bought a house because everyone said it was a smart investment, and I've regretted it ever since." She looked down at her hands. "I just don't make good decisions."

"I'm curious," I said. "Were there any warning signs along the way? Any moments where some part of you hesitated or felt uncertain about these choices?"

Veronica was quiet for a moment, then nodded slowly. "With my ex, I remember this hollow feeling in my stomach whenever we talked about the future. With the job, I actually had trouble sleeping the night before I accepted the offer. And with the house…" She trailed off.

"With the house?" I prompted gently.

"With the house, I remember standing in the empty living room after the inspection, and suddenly feeling like I couldn't breathe. But the market was hot, my friends were all buying places, and the mortgage broker was pushing for an answer. So I just ignored that feeling and signed the papers."

"So in each of these situations, there was a part of you that actually did know something wasn't right," I observed. "A physical sensation, an emotional response, an intuitive hesitation, a spiritual knowing. But you didn't trust those signals."

"I didn't even really register them as signals," Veronica admitted. "I thought they were just anxiety or cold feet. I trusted what everyone else was telling me instead."

This exchange captures something important to recognize in people who can identify with this: the disconnect between their inner knowing and their conscious decisions, much like an internal spiritual void. They've often been taught—directly or indirectly—to distrust their own experience and defer to external authorities, whether those authorities are parents, partners, experts, or cultural norms.

The result is a kind of inner estrangement, where we become strangers to our own wisdom and intuition. We stop listening to the subtle (and sometimes not-so-subtle) signals from our bodies, emotions, and intuition. Instead, we place our trust in what others tell us we should think, feel, want, or do.

Rebuilding self-trust after years or decades of this inner estrangement isn't simple. It requires a fundamental shift in how we relate to our own experience—learning to value and attend to our internal signals rather than automatically dismissing or overriding them in favor of external guidance.

THE FOUNDATION OF SELF-TRUST

"I think I'm fundamentally confused about what it even means to trust myself," Veronica told me during our next session. "Is it about following my feelings? But feelings can be misleading, right? Is it about trusting my thinking? But my thoughts can be irrational sometimes. What part of myself am I supposed to trust?"

This question—what aspect of our complex inner landscape deserves our trust—is crucial. Self-trust isn't about blindly following every feeling, thought, or impulse that arises. It's about developing a more nuanced relationship with our inner experience, learning to discern which aspects of that experience offer reliable guidance and which might be misleading. This is often where a person's faith plays a role.

In my work with clients, I've found it helpful to think about self-trust as resting on three interconnected foundations:

1. EMBODIED AWARENESS

As we covered earlier in the book, our bodies often know things before our conscious minds do. Physical sensations—tension, constriction, hollowness, heaviness, expansion, lightness—can provide valuable information about what's right for us and what isn't. These sensations aren't random; they're part of our organism's intelligence, signaling alignment or misalignment with our authentic needs and values.

Veronica's hollow feeling when discussing the future with her ex, her insomnia before accepting the job, her difficulty breathing in the empty house—these were all embodied signals trying to communicate important information. But because she'd been taught to prioritize external validation over internal wisdom, she'd dismissed these signals as meaningless anxiety.

2. EMOTIONAL INTELLIGENCE

Our emotions, when we learn to work with them rather than being hijacked by them, offer another source of trustworthy guidance. Emotions are messengers, providing information about our needs, values, and boundaries. Anger might signal a boundary violation. Sadness might indicate a loss that matters to us. Fear might reveal something we need to protect. Joy might highlight what genuinely nourishes us.

The challenge is distinguishing between primary, authentic emotions and secondary, reactive ones. Primary emotions arise directly in response to a situation and offer clean information. Secondary emotions are our reactions to our primary emotions and often reflect conditioning rather than authentic responses.

For Veronica, learning to distinguish between authentic emotional responses and conditioned reactions became an important part of rebuilding self-trust. She began to recognize that her anxiety about disappointing others was a secondary emotion, often masking primary feelings like discontentment or sadness that contained valuable information about her true needs.

3. VALUES CLARITY

The third foundation of self-trust is clarity about our authentic values—as we've discussed previously, not the values we've inherited or adopted to gain approval, but the principles that genuinely matter to us when we're connected to our deeper understanding. For many, this is guided by faith in God.

When we act in alignment with our authentic values, we build trust in ourselves through lived experience. Each time we honor what truly matters to us, even in small ways, we strengthen our confidence in our capacity to make choices that serve our well-being and integrity.

For Veronica, exploring her authentic values revealed some surprising insights. While she'd built her life around the values of achievement, security, and social approval, her moments of greatest fulfillment came when she was expressing creativity, contributing meaningfully to others, and experiencing freedom and spaciousness in her life. She knew this was how she was designed from the beginning.

"I've been climbing a ladder that's leaning against the wrong wall," she realized in one session. "No wonder none of these 'successful' choices have felt right—they're successful according to values that aren't actually mine."

These three foundations—embodied awareness, emotional intelligence, and values clarity—work together to create a reliable internal guidance system. But accessing this guidance requires a fundamental shift in attention: turning inward to our own experience before turning outward for validation or direction.

STAYING WITH YOUR OWN EXPERIENCE

"I noticed something strange this week," Veronica told me about two months into our work together. "I was having lunch with my friend Megan, who was complaining about her job. Before I even registered what I was feeling about what she was saying, I was already crafting the perfect supportive response. It's like I completely bypassed my own reaction and went straight to managing hers."

"That's an important observation," I acknowledged. "What happened when you noticed that pattern?"

"I tried something different. I just paused and asked myself, 'What am I actually feeling right now as I listen to Megan?' And I realized I was feeling a mix of things—some sympathy, yes, but also some irritation because she complains about this job every time we meet but never does anything to change it. And some anxiety because I felt responsible for making her feel better."

"And did you express any of that to her?" I asked.

Veronica shook her head. "No, not directly. But I did stop myself from jumping into fix-it mode. I just listened and acknowledged what she was saying without trying to solve her problem or manage her feelings. It felt…different. More honest somehow, even though I didn't share my irritation."

This subtle shift—pausing to register your own experience before responding to others—is one of the most powerful practices for rebuilding self-trust. Many of us have become so externally oriented that we habitually bypass our own reactions, focusing immediately on how we should respond to others rather than checking in with ourselves first.

This bypassing creates a disconnect between our authentic experience and our outward behavior. Over time, this disconnect erodes self-trust, as we come to feel that our actions aren't genuinely aligned with our internal reality.

The practice of staying with your own experience doesn't mean you always express everything you're feeling. It simply means you acknowledge your authentic response before deciding how to engage. This internal acknowledgment creates congruence between your inner and outer worlds, even when you choose not to share certain aspects of your experience.

This practice gradually transformed Veronica's relationships. She began to notice how often she'd been overriding her own needs and feelings to accommodate others, not because they demanded it, but because she'd never learned to value her own experience as worthy of consideration.

"I realized I've been treating myself as an afterthought in my own life," she told me. "Like my only value is in what I can do for others, not in who I am or what I need."

THE PRACTICE

Rebuilding self-trust doesn't happen overnight or through grand gestures. It develops through consistent small actions that honor your experience, needs, and values. These actions might feel uncomfortable at first, especially if you've spent years prioritizing external validation over internal wisdom. But each step, however small, strengthens your confidence in your capacity to guide your own life.

Here are some of the practices that helped Veronica rebuild trust in herself:

THE BODY CHECK-IN

Several times throughout the day, Veronica would pause and simply notice what was happening in her body. She'd scan from head to toe, observing physical sensations without trying to change them. Where was she holding tension? What parts felt open and relaxed? Was her breathing shallow or deep? Was there a knot in her stomach or a tightness in her throat?

This simple practice helped her reestablish connection with her body's wisdom. She began to recognize patterns—how certain people or situations reliably created constriction, while others generated a sense of expansion and ease. These patterns provided valuable information about what was and wasn't aligned with her authentic needs.

"I used to think my tension headaches were just from stress," Veronica told me. "Now I realize they often come when I'm agreeing to something I don't actually want to do. My body knows before my mind is willing to admit it."

THE DESIRE EXPERIMENT

I suggested that Veronica experiment with small, low-stakes choices based solely on what she genuinely wanted in the moment, without considering what she "should" want or what others might prefer.

"This Saturday, just for the morning, make choices based on what you actually desire," I suggested. "What time do you want to wake up? What would you enjoy for breakfast? What activity would feel good to you? Just for a few hours, let desire be your guide."

This experiment often reveals how disconnected we've become from our authentic preferences. Many clients discover they don't know what they want when "should" is removed from the equation. This not-knowing is an important recognition. You can't trust yourself if you don't know yourself.

For Veronica, the desire experiment led to some surprising discoveries. She realized she'd been forcing herself to attend crowded exercise classes because she thought she "should" enjoy them, when she actually preferred solitary walks. She discovered she didn't really like the fancy coffee drinks she routinely ordered but had been choosing them because they seemed sophisticated.

"It sounds so small and silly," she said, "but realizing I don't have to pretend to like oat milk lattes was strangely liberating. What else have I been pretending to want without even realizing it?"

THE MICRO-DECISION PRACTICE

Building on her growing clarity about her values and preferences, Veronica began practicing self-trust through micro-decisions—small, everyday choices where she deliberately checked in with her internal guidance rather than defaulting to external validation or the "should story" in her head.

When invited to an event, she'd pause and ask: Does this align with how I want to spend my time and energy? When considering a purchase, she'd check: Is this something I genuinely want, or am

I buying it to impress others or fill an emotional void? When faced with a work opportunity, she'd consider: Does this align with my authentic values, or just with external definitions of success?

The key to this practice was making decisions from a place of connection to herself rather than reactivity to others. This didn't mean ignoring practical constraints or others' needs. It meant including her own experience as a valid and important consideration in the decision-making process.

Over time, these micro-decisions built Veronica's confidence in her ability to make choices that honored her authentic self. Each time she trusted her internal guidance and experienced a positive outcome, her faith in herself grew stronger.

THE BOUNDARY EXPERIMENT

As Veronica's self-trust grew, she began experimenting with more explicit boundaries in her relationships. This wasn't about building walls, but about clearly communicating her needs and limits from a place of self-connection rather than resentment or reactivity.

"I told my mother I would be coming home for part of the week of Christmas this year, but unable to stay the entire week," Veronica reported in one session. "In the past, I would have just gone along with her expectations, even though those long visits are exhausting for me. But this time, I acknowledged my own needs and communicated them clearly."

"How did that go?" I asked.

"She was disappointed at first, but she didn't fall apart or disown me," Veronica said with a small smile. "And what really surprised me was how I felt afterward—not guilty, like I expected, but relieved and actually more loving toward her. It's like by honoring my own needs, I created more authentic space for the relationship."

When we honor our authentic experience and needs, we often become more genuinely available for connection, not less. The energy previously spent on resentment, people-pleasing, and disconnection from self becomes available for real presence with others.

THE CHALLENGE OF DIFFERENTIATION

About six months into our work together, Veronica encountered a significant challenge to her growing self-trust. She'd begun dating someone new, a man named Kyle, who seemed, on the surface, to offer everything her previous relationship had lacked: emotional availability, clear communication, and genuine interest in her well-being.

"But something feels off, and I can't figure out what it is," she told me. "On paper, he's perfect. My friends all think he's amazing. But there's this hesitation I feel, and I don't know if I should trust it or if it's just my old patterns acting up."

This scenario—where our internal signals conflict with external validation—provides perhaps the most important testing ground for self-trust. It's relatively easy to trust ourselves when others agree with our perceptions. The real challenge comes when our experience diverges from external consensus.

"Tell me more about this hesitation," I encouraged. "What does it feel like? When does it show up?"

Veronica thought for a moment. "It's subtle. A slight constriction in my chest sometimes when we're together. A sense that I'm performing more than I want to be. He's very certain about what he wants, which I thought I'd find reassuring, but sometimes, it feels like there isn't room for my uncertainty or process."

"And how have you been responding to these signals?" I asked.

"I've been telling myself they don't mean anything," she admitted. "That I'm just not used to someone being so direct and available. That I'm looking for problems because I'm scared of intimacy. All the things my friends would say if I mentioned my reservations."

This is the crux of the self-trust challenge: discerning when our internal signals are offering wisdom versus when they're reflecting old wounds or fears. This discernment isn't about ignoring either possibility, but about staying present with our experience long enough to understand what it's communicating.

"What if we approached this with curiosity rather than judgment?" I suggested. "Not assuming these signals mean you should end the relationship, but also not dismissing them as meaningless?"

Veronica nodded. "That makes sense. But how do I tell the difference between wisdom and fear?"

"Wisdom tends to feel clear and centered, even when it's delivering uncomfortable truths," I offered. "Fear tends to feel contracted, urgent, and absolute. Wisdom acknowledges complexity; fear demands black-and-white certainty. But the most reliable way to discern between them is to stay with your experience rather than abandoning it."

Over the next few weeks, Veronica practiced staying with her experience in the relationship with Kyle. Rather than either acting on her hesitation immediately or dismissing it entirely, she remained curious about what it might be trying to communicate.

What emerged was nuanced: Kyle was indeed emotionally available and caring, but his certainty about what he wanted sometimes left little room for Veronica's more exploratory process. His vision for the relationship, while clear and positive, didn't fully align with the direction her life was taking. The hesitation she felt wasn't about fear of intimacy, but about a subtle misalignment in values and approach that mattered to her.

"I think in the past, I would have either ignored these signals and tried to make myself fit his vision, or I would have run away because the discomfort felt threatening," Veronica reflected. "But this time, I stayed with my experience long enough to understand what it was telling me. And that understanding let me have an honest conversation with him about what I was noticing."

The relationship ultimately didn't continue, but the way it ended reflected Veronica's growing self-trust. Rather than either abandoning herself to maintain the connection or fleeing to avoid vulnerability, she engaged authentically from a place of connection to her own experience.

"It wasn't about him being wrong or bad, or about me being broken," she told me. "It was about trusting that my experience contained important information, even when that information wasn't what others might have expected or what I initially hoped to find."

SELF-TRUST IS HARD WORK

Self-trust is a practice rather than a permanent achievement. We don't develop self-trust once and for all; we cultivate it through ongoing commitment to honoring our experience, even when doing so feels challenging or countercultural.

Let me be clear that the practice of self-trust doesn't mean we never seek input or guidance from others. It means we receive that input without abandoning our own perspective in the process. We might consider others' viewpoints, weigh their expertise or experience, and allow their insights to inform our thinking. But we remain the ultimate authority on our own lives, considering external wisdom rather than being controlled by it.

For Veronica, this integration became evident in how she approached major life decisions. When considering a career transition, she consulted mentors and researched various paths, but she ultimately made her choice based on what aligned with her authentic values and needs, not what others thought would be most impressive or secure.

"The difference now is that I'm making decisions with myself, not despite myself," she explained in our final session. "I'm not perfect at it. I still get swayed by what others think sometimes. But I catch it quicker, and I know how to find my way back to my own perspective."

The practice of self-trust extends far beyond individual decision-making. When we learn to honor our own experience—to stay with ourselves before turning outward for validation or direction—we fundamentally change how we show up in all aspects of life.

In relationships, self-trust allows us to engage from a place of authenticity rather than avoidance, performance, or people-pleasing. We can be genuinely present with others because we're not ignoring ourselves in the process. This creates space for others to be authentic and thus the possibility for real intimacy—the meeting of two authentic selves rather than the intersection of two constructed personas.

In work, self-trust enables us to contribute our unique perspectives and talents rather than playing out a script or simply conforming to expectations. We can take appropriate risks, set meaningful boundaries, and align our efforts with our authentic values rather than external metrics of success.

In creative endeavors, self-trust gives us access to our distinctive vision and voice. Instead of imitating what's already been done or creating primarily for approval, we can express what genuinely moves and matters to us, contributing something original to the world.

Perhaps most fundamentally, self-trust changes our relationship with uncertainty and complexity. When we trust our capacity to stay with our own experience—to sense what we sense, feel what we feel, and value what we value—we become less dependent on external certainty or validation. We can navigate ambiguity with more grace, holding the tension of not-knowing without abandoning ourselves in the process.

This doesn't mean we never feel lost or confused. It means that even in our lostness, we remain present with ourselves rather than grasping for someone else to tell us who we are or what we should do.

As you continue your own self-discovery expedition, I encourage you to practice this fundamental skill of staying with your own experience before turning outward. Notice when you bypass your authentic response in favor of managing others' perceptions or meeting external expectations. Experiment with small acts of self-trust, gradually building confidence in your capacity to guide your own life from a place of genuine self-connection.

The path of self-trust isn't always easy, especially in a culture that often prioritizes external validation over internal wisdom. But it offers something precious: the opportunity to live the life that is really yours, not the one scripted by others in your core narrative or in your present situation. You will discover that the most enjoyable thing to do on the planet is to just be who you really are from the inside out rather than from the outside in, guided by your authentic values and experience rather than by others' expectations or demands. This is what it means to answer: "Where am I in this?"

CHAPTER 15

FINDING YOUR STANDARDS OF SUCCESS

"**B**Y ANY OBJECTIVE measure, I should be happy," Hunter said, leaning back in his chair with a sigh. "I go to an amazing school, hold positions in some of the top on-campus organizations, I'm dating the girl most guys envy—all the boxes checked. So why do I feel like I'm failing?"

Hunter was a student at his top choice university. He initially sought therapy for what he described as "unexplainable discontent." On paper, his life looked enviable. He held a great position in an organization on campus, his grades were on-point, and he was in a stable, long-term relationship. Yet despite meeting all these conventional markers of success, he felt increasingly hollow and restless.

"Tell me more about these 'objective measures' you mentioned," I encouraged. "What are the metrics you're using to evaluate your life?"

Hunter thought for a moment. "The usual stuff, I guess. Career advancement. Financial security. Relationship stability. The things everyone wants."

"Everyone?" I asked gently.

"Well, most people," he amended. "The normal benchmarks of a successful life."

"And who defined these benchmarks for you?"

The question seemed to catch him off guard. "I don't know. Society? My parents, maybe? It's just what you're supposed to do, isn't it? Get the degree, climb the ladder, buy the house, settle down."

"What if there isn't a single 'supposed to' that applies to everyone?" I suggested. "What if the metrics that matter most are actually unique to each person?"

Hunter looked skeptical. "That sounds nice in theory, but in the real world, there are certain standards everyone is measured by."

"There are certainly common external metrics," I acknowledged. "And they can be powerful. But I'm wondering if those external measures are aligned with what matters most to you personally. If they were, would achieving them leave you feeling this empty?"

Underneath Hunter's "unexplainable discontent" was a common misalignment—he had achieved success according to external standards while neglecting to define what success meant to him.

Many of us can relate because we move through life measuring ourselves against metrics we've inherited or absorbed rather than consciously chosen. We chase promotions, income thresholds, relationship milestones, or social validation without stopping to question whether these achievements align with our authentic values and desires.

The result is what we sometimes call "success dysfunction"—the hollow feeling that comes when we've climbed the ladder only to discover it was leaning against the wrong wall. We've measured up according to external standards but failed to define or even honor our own internal metrics of meaning and fulfillment.

"I've been thinking about what you said last session," Hunter told me when we next met. "About whether the standards I've been measuring myself against actually align with what matters to me."

"What's come up for you around that?" I asked.

"I realized I've never really questioned which metrics matter to me," he said. "It's like I've been running a race without ever asking if it's a race I want to run."

This unconscious adoption of external metrics is something I've observed in many clients. We absorb standards of success and worth from our families, education systems, peer groups, and broader culture, often without realizing how powerfully these adopted measures shape our choices and self-evaluation.

External metrics are not inherently problematic. A good salary can provide security and opportunity. Recognition can validate our efforts and contributions. Material comforts can potentially enhance our quality of life. The issue isn't with these achievements themselves, but with mistaking them for universal measures of worth or fulfillment.

The problems arise when we:

1. **Adopt Metrics Without Examination:** We pursue goals without questioning whether they align with our authentic values and desires.

2. **Mistake the Map for the Territory:** We confuse external markers of success with actual fulfillment or meaning.

3. **Ignore Personal Cost:** We achieve external success while compromising our well-being, relationships, or authentic expression.

4. **Perpetually Move the Goalposts:** External metrics often shift once achieved, creating a never-ending pursuit rather than a sense of arrival or sufficiency.

5. **Disconnect From Embodied Experience:** We override our felt sense of alignment or misalignment in favor of objective "proof" of success.

For Hunter, the pursuit of conventional success metrics had come with significant costs. Despite his academic and social achievements, he found little meaning in his day-to-day life. His assignments, projects, and social commitments left him chronically exhausted. His relationship was stable but increasingly distant, as both partners focused more on maintaining the appearance of success than on genuine connection.

"I keep thinking I should be grateful," Hunter told me. "So many people would love to have what I have. But honestly? Most days I just feel trapped by all these achievements."

This sentiment—feeling trapped by one's own success—is a common consequence of measuring ourselves primarily by external standards. We build lives that look impressive from the outside but feel confining from within. We achieve the metrics we've been taught to value, only to discover they don't deliver the fulfillment we expected.

The alternative isn't to reject all external measures or to abandon ambition. It's to consciously develop personal metrics that align with our authentic values and desires, using these self-defined standards as our primary compass while maintaining a more balanced relationship with external validation.

DEVELOPING PERSONAL METRICS

"So if I shouldn't be measuring myself by the usual standards, what should I be measuring instead?" Hunter asked during our third session.

"I'm not suggesting you shouldn't consider conventional metrics at all," I clarified. "Just that they work better as secondary measures rather than primary ones. The question is: What primary metrics would actually reflect what matters most to you?"

Hunter looked genuinely perplexed. "I don't even know how to figure that out. It's like I've been following a script for so long, I'm not sure what I'd write for myself if I had the chance."

This is where the real work begins: the process of developing personal metrics that are genuinely aligned with our authentic values, desires, and sense of meaning. It's not a quick or simple process, but it's transformative in its impact on how we experience our lives and measure our growth.

Here are some of the approaches that helped Hunter begin to define his own metrics.

EXAMINE THE ORIGIN STORY BEHIND YOUR CURRENT METRICS

We started by exploring the origins of the metrics Hunter had been using to evaluate his life and worth. Where did these standards come from? What messages had he received growing up about what constituted success or failure? Who had defined these benchmarks, and why had they held such power in his life?

"My father was always very focused on status and security," Hunter revealed as we traced these influences. "He grew up poor and was determined that his children would never face that insecurity. Achievement was everything—the right schools, the right jobs, the right neighborhood."

"And how did that shape your understanding of success?" I asked.

"Success meant approval and security," Hunter said after reflecting for a moment. "Proving my worth through achievements that no one could take away. Making sure I was valued enough that I wouldn't be discarded."

This exploration revealed something important: The external metrics Hunter had been pursuing weren't random. They were connected to core emotional needs for security and validation that originated in his family system. Understanding this connection didn't invalidate those needs, but it created space to consider whether his current approach was the most effective way to meet them.

"I wonder if there might be other ways to create security in your life," I suggested. "Ways that feel more aligned with who you are now, not just who you needed to be then."

RECONNECT WITH INTRINSIC MOTIVATION

Next, we worked on reconnecting Hunter with his intrinsic motivations: the activities, qualities, and experiences that felt inherently rewarding to him, regardless of external recognition or reward.

One powerful approach was the "flow inventory"—identifying times when he experienced the state of flow, described by psychologist Mihaly Csikszentmihalyi as being so absorbed and engaged in an activity that time seems to disappear. These flow experiences often point to areas of natural alignment and intrinsic motivation.

"I realize I haven't felt that sense of flow while at school lately," Hunter noted after this exploration. "But I do feel it sometimes when I'm cooking elaborate meals on the weekends, or when I was helping my friend with his science project last month. There's something about creating something tangible, something I can see and touch, that gives me a satisfaction I never get from rigid assignments and assessments."

Another approach was examining what Hunter naturally valued and enjoyed when he was younger, before external expectations had shaped his choices. What had drawn his interest and enthusiasm before he learned to perform for validation?

"I was obsessed with building things," he recalled. "Legos, model planes, tree houses—anything I could design and construct with my hands. My parents saw it as a cute hobby, but what they really praised was my grades and achievements. So eventually I just focused on what got me the approval."

These explorations revealed aspects of Hunter's authentic interests and values that had been submerged beneath years of externally oriented achievement. They provided clues to what might constitute more personally meaningful metrics of engagement and satisfaction in his life.

CLARIFY YOUR VALUES

With greater awareness of both the origin story behind his external metrics and his intrinsic motivations, Hunter was ready to begin defining more value-aligned standards for measuring his life and choices.

We started with a values clarification process, helping him identify what truly mattered to him—not what he'd been told should matter, but what resonated at a deeper level. This exploration revealed core values including creativity, autonomy, contribution, and connection.

Then came the crucial step: translating these values into concrete, measurable ways of evaluating his life and choices. For each value, we developed specific questions and indicators that could serve as personal metrics:

For creativity:

- Am I regularly making or building things that engage my imagination?
- How often do I approach problems in novel ways rather than defaulting to established procedures?
- Do I have space in my life for experimentation and play?

For autonomy:

- How much of my daily schedule reflects my own priorities versus others' expectations?
- Do I make decisions from internal clarity or external pressure?
- Am I able to set boundaries that protect my essential needs and values?

For contribution:

- Can I see the tangible impact of my work?
- Am I using my specific gifts and talents in service of something I believe matters?
- Does my contribution align with my authentic values, not just organizational metrics?

For connection:

- Do I have relationships where I can know and be fully known and accepted?
- How often do I engage in genuine, present-moment connection versus performative interaction?
- Am I nurturing the relationships that matter most to me, not just those that offer strategic advantage?

Hunter's personal metrics were redefined to be in alignment with his authentic values. They could now deliver the fulfillment he had always sought from them.

"What strikes me about these metrics is that they're about the quality of my experience, not just observable outcomes," Hunter noted as we developed them. "They're measuring things that matter to me subjectively, not just what looks impressive to others."

"That's an important distinction," I agreed. "External metrics tend to focus almost exclusively on outcomes and appearances. Personal metrics often include the felt experience of the experience itself—how engaged, authentic, and aligned you feel in the process, not just what you achieve at the end. It is truly finding where YOU are in this."

IDENTIFY YOUR "ENOUGH" POINTS

One of the most powerful aspects of developing personal metrics is establishing what I call "enough" points—the thresholds at which you can genuinely say "This is sufficient" rather than perpetually chasing more.

External metrics often lack these enough points. There's always a higher income to earn, another degree to pursue, a more prestigious position to attain. This absence of clear sufficiency creates a treadmill effect, where achievement never leads to lasting satisfaction because the goal continuously expands.

For Hunter, defining enough points in various areas of his life became a transformative practice:

"I realized I passed my 'enough points' for extracurricular endeavors," he told me. "What I am involved in now is well beyond what I need for my satisfaction. But I never stopped to acknowledge that because everyone around me just keeps pushing for more. Once I recognized I had enough, it changed how I evaluated new opportunities and options. I could start prioritizing meaning and enjoyment rather than just resume building."

This concept of enough is about consciously defining sufficiency in alignment with your actual needs and values, so you can focus your energy on what truly enhances your life rather than endlessly pursuing more of what you already have enough of.

Some areas where defining enough points can be particularly powerful include:

- **Material Possessions:** What level of comfort and convenience genuinely enhances your well-being, versus creating additional maintenance demands?
- **Work Achievement:** What level of success provides appropriate challenge and recognition without comprising your entire identity?

- **Social Approval:** How much external validation is helpful before it becomes an addiction that disconnects you from your authentic preferences?
- **Information:** When does additional research or knowledge empower your decisions versus becoming a form of procrastination?

For each area, the enough point will be unique to your values and circumstances. The key is consciously establishing these thresholds rather than defaulting to the cultural assumption that more is always better. Make no mistake, this is easier said than done. Cultural assumptions run deep and those expectations scream loudly to us!

RECONNECTION WITH YOUR EMBODIED EXPERIENCE

Perhaps the most fundamental shift in moving from external to personal metrics is reconnecting with your embodied experience as a valid source of information about success and alignment.

External metrics are primarily cognitive and comparative—they exist in the realm of thought and social evaluation. Personal metrics, while they can include cognitive elements, are often more deeply rooted in embodied experience—how you feel in your body, emotions, and spirit when you're living in alignment with what truly matters to you.

For Hunter, developing these embodied success indicators meant learning to recognize and trust the physical and emotional signals that accompanied authentic engagement and fulfillment.

"I noticed something strange recently," he told me. "I was in a meeting for an on-campus organization, presenting a new initiative I'd developed that focused on a process I was proposing rather than just recognition. My heart was beating faster, but not from anxiety like usual—more from excitement. I felt energized rather than drained. My voice was stronger, more confident. It was like my body was telling me 'this matters' in a way I could physically feel."

These embodied indicators—energy, enthusiasm, presence, ease, flow, authentic engagement—provide powerful real-time feedback about alignment with our deeper values and purpose. Unlike external metrics, which often require waiting for others' evaluation or achieving specific outcomes, embodied metrics offer immediate information about whether our current choices and activities are aligned with what truly matters to us.

For Hunter, learning to recognize and trust these embodied signals became an essential practice in evaluating his life and choices according to more authentic standards. It didn't mean abandoning all external measures; it meant giving priority to his lived experience rather than sacrificing that experience for the sake of appearances or others' approval.

LIVING BY YOUR OWN METRICS

Over the course of our work together, Hunter gradually shifted from measuring his life primarily by external standards to using his self-defined metrics as his principal guide. This shift wasn't about rejecting all conventional forms of success, but about putting them in proper perspective—as potential means to deeper ends rather than ends in themselves.

About eight months into our work, Hunter made a significant degree change that reflected this evolution. He didn't abandon his career desires, but he chose a slightly different plan. He developed a schedule that allowed him to launch a small furniture-making business on the side—a venture that engaged his long-neglected love of creating tangible things with his hands.

"Some of my family think I'm crazy for 'shifting focus' when I was on track for another internship," he told me. "But for the first time in years, I actually look forward to the things I am working on. I'm making things I'm proud of, developing skills that matter to me, not just adding bullet points to my resume."

Personal metrics often lead to choices that others don't immediately understand or validate. When you're measuring your life by standards that align with your authentic values rather than conventional expectations, your decisions may seem puzzling or even foolish to those still operating primarily by external metrics.

"My father is particularly confused by my choices," Hunter admitted. "He keeps asking when I'm going back to my 'real plan' full-time, as if my plan of finishing my degree while growing my furniture business isn't a real plan. I don't think he'll ever fully understand, and that's okay. I'm not living his life; I'm living mine."

This capacity to maintain conviction in your own metrics, even when they aren't validated by others, represents a crucial aspect of authentic living. It means developing sufficient inner authority to distinguish between helpful input and projections or expectations that don't align with your authentic values.

This growing inner authority extended beyond Hunter's career into his relationship. He and his partner had difficult but necessary conversations about their different priorities and values, ultimately deciding to go their separate ways, a painful but ultimately liberating choice that created space for both to pursue more authentic paths.

He also decided to resign from one of his positions in an on-campus organization. While he enjoyed the people involved, he was not impassioned by the work. By doing so, he freed up time that he spent building what was more aligned with his authentic metrics.

"On paper, these changes probably look like steps backward," Hunter reflected. "No longer in as many positions on campus, not dating anyone, and not going for all of the corporate internships. But by the metrics that actually matter to me now, my life is richer than it's ever been. I'm creating things I care about. I have more authentic connections. I'm making choices from a place of alignment rather than expectation. That's success by my definition, even if it doesn't impress at a party."

This shift—from living to impress others to living in alignment with your own authentic metrics—doesn't happen overnight or without challenges. It's a practice that requires ongoing attention to both internal signals and external influences, continually recalibrating to ensure your choices reflect what truly matters to you.

THE PRACTICE

If you recognize yourself in Hunter's initial situation—achieving external success while feeling internally disconnected or unfulfilled—here are some practical approaches for developing and implementing your own authentic metrics:

1. EXAMINE THE STORY BEHIND YOUR CURRENT METRICS.

Start by examining the standards you're currently using to evaluate your life and choices. Make a list of the metrics you consciously or unconsciously apply, considering areas like:

- career and work achievement
- financial status
- relationships and family
- physical appearance and health
- home and possessions
- social status and recognition
- personal development and spiritual growth

For each metric, ask yourself:

- Where did this standard come from?
- Does achieving it create lasting fulfillment or meaning for me?
- What needs or values is it attempting to meet?

- Are there other ways to meet those needs that might feel more aligned?

This audit often reveals how many of our current metrics were inherited or absorbed rather than consciously chosen, creating awareness that opens the possibility for more intentional standards. This allows for discovering where am I in these metrics.

2. Reconnect with intrinsic motivation—find the flow.

Identify moments in your life when you've felt most alive, engaged, and fulfilled. These peak experiences often reveal what truly matters to you beneath the layers of conditioning and expectation.

For each peak experience, explore:

- What was happening in this moment?
- What values were being expressed or honored?
- What qualities were present in your experience—connection, creativity, challenge, service, adventure, or something else?
- How might these qualities be translated into ongoing metrics for measuring your life?

These peak experiences provide clues to what constitutes genuine success and fulfillment according to your authentic nature, not external definitions.

3. Clarify your values.

Beyond conventional success measures, define metrics that capture what creates genuine meaning and fulfillment for you personally.

Consider questions like:

- How often am I fully engaged in activities that matter to me?
- To what extent am I using my specific gifts and talents?

- How frequently do I experience genuine connection with others?
- When do I feel a sense of purpose or contribution?
- In what contexts do I feel most authentically myself?

These meaning metrics provide a more holistic and personally relevant way to evaluate your life than conventional achievement standards alone.

4. IDENTIFY YOUR "ENOUGH" POINTS.

For various areas of your life, consciously establish what constitutes "enough" according to your actual needs and values, not comparative or aspirational standards.

Ask yourself:

- What level of income or financial security would genuinely meet my needs?
- How much space, comfort, or convenience do I truly need in my living situation?
- What level of recognition or validation enhances my well-being?
- How much information or preparation do I need to move forward with confidence?

Setting these enough points provides clear sufficiency thresholds that prevent the endless pursuit of more, creating space to focus on what genuinely enhances your life.

5. RECONNECT WITH YOUR EMBODIED EXPERIENCE.

Learn to recognize and trust the physical, emotional, and spiritual signals that indicate alignment or misalignment with your authentic values and desires.

Pay attention to:

- when you feel energized versus drained

- where you experience ease versus tension or resistance
- when time seems to flow versus drag
- what brings a sense of expansion versus contraction
- when you feel authentically engaged versus performing

These embodied signals provide real-time feedback about alignment that's often more reliable than external validation or abstract principles.

6. IMPLEMENT REGULAR REVIEW PRACTICES.

Create consistent opportunities to evaluate your life according to your personal metrics, not just external achievements or social comparisons.

This might include:

- weekly reflection on moments of alignment and misalignment
- monthly review of choices and activities against your core values
- quarterly assessment of progress toward personally meaningful goals
- annual "life audit" examining how various areas of your life reflect what matters most to you

These regular reviews help maintain awareness of your authentic metrics amid the constant pressure of external standards and expectations.

When we're primarily measuring ourselves by external standards, we tend to relate to others through the lens of comparison, competition, or strategic advantage. We see relationships as means to ends rather than ends in themselves. We're constantly positioning ourselves relative to others rather than genuinely connecting with them.

But when we develop clear personal metrics based on our authentic values, we create the foundation for more genuine presence and connection. We no longer need others to validate our worth or choices because we have our own internal compass. This inner security allows us to engage more authentically, without the constant self-consciousness that comes from measuring ourselves against external standards.

This freedom manifested in a transformation of Hunter's relationships. He developed deeper friendships based on shared interests and values rather than professional networking. He began volunteering with a program teaching woodworking to at-risk youth, finding meaning in passing on skills he valued to young people who might not otherwise have such opportunities.

"I used to evaluate relationships based on what they could do for me professionally or how they reflected on my status," he admitted. "Now I value them for the actual connection and meaning they bring to my life. It's a completely different way of being with people."

This shift—from relating to others as mirrors reflecting our status or worth to engaging with them as genuine connections—represents one of the most significant benefits of defining your own metrics. When you're clear about what matters to you and measure yourself accordingly, you're freed from the constant need for external validation that turns relationships into performances rather than authentic engagements.

The freedom of personal metrics extends beyond relationships to your experience of time and choice as well. When you're measuring your life by standards that align with your authentic values, you approach decisions differently—not by calculating their impact on your external status, but by considering their alignment with what truly matters to you.

"I make choices differently now," Hunter noted. "I used to constantly ask myself, 'How will this look? What will people think? Will this advance my position?' Now I ask, 'Does this align with what I value? Will this allow me to create, connect, or contribute in ways that feel meaningful? Does this honor my enough points or push me into unnecessary excess?'"

This shift does not necessarily make decisions easier, but because the criteria are clearer and more personally meaningful, you're no longer trying to optimize for multiple external standards that may conflict with your authentic desires. You're making choices in alignment with your own consciously defined metrics of what constitutes a well-lived life.

CLOSING

CHAPTER 16

THE ONGOING NATURE OF SELF-DISCOVERY

"I **THINK I'VE FINALLY** figured myself out," Claire announced with satisfaction as she settled into her chair for what would be one of our final sessions after nearly two years of work together.

I smiled. "Tell me more about that."

"Well, I know my core values now. I understand my relationship patterns. I can recognize when I'm acting from old wounds versus authentic desires. I've rebuilt trust in myself. I've even created my own metrics for success." She ticked these accomplishments off on her fingers. "I feel like I've finally arrived."

"That's wonderful," I acknowledged. "You've done remarkable work."

Claire nodded, clearly pleased with herself. Then she paused, noticing something in my expression. "Why do I feel like there's a 'but' coming?"

I laughed. "Not a 'but' exactly. More of an 'and.' All of this self-knowledge is genuinely valuable. And...it's not the end."

"What do you mean?" Claire asked, her brow furrowing slightly.

"I mean that knowing yourself isn't a destination you reach once and for all. It's more like driving a car. You don't fill the gas tank once and declare, 'Done!' You monitor the dashboard, refuel regularly, adjust course as needed, and remain aware of changing conditions both inside and outside the vehicle."

Claire considered this. "So you're saying all this work I've done is…temporary?"

"Not temporary," I clarified. "Foundational. You've built something real and valuable. But self-discovery isn't a one-time achievement—it's an ongoing practice. The person you are at forty isn't the person you were at twenty, and it won't be the person you'll be at sixty. You're constantly evolving, and your self-knowledge needs to evolve too."

Claire sat back, taking this in. "That's a little deflating, to be honest. I thought I was nearing the finish line."

"I understand that." I nodded. "Our culture loves finish lines— clear markers of completion and achievement. But when it comes to knowing yourself, there isn't a point where you can say, 'I'm done now, I've figured it all out.' And honestly, would you want there to be?"

"What do you mean?"

"I mean, what if the ongoing nature of self-discovery isn't a burden but a gift? What if the continual unfolding of who you are is actually one of the great adventures of being alive?"

Many clients reach this same point in their path of self-discovery: the point where they've gained significant insights and made meaningful changes, and they're ready to declare, "Mission accomplished." It's a natural desire. We want to feel we've completed something, solved the puzzle, and reached the destination.

But the truth about knowing yourself is both more challenging and more liberating than that. Self-discovery isn't a project to complete; it's a practice to maintain. It's not about arriving at a fixed understanding of who you are, but about developing the awareness, curiosity, and compassion to continuously discover yourself anew as you grow and change throughout your life. It's about showing up!

THE DASHBOARD, NOT THE DESTINATION

I often use the metaphor of driving a car to help clients understand the ongoing nature of self-discovery. When you're driving, you don't set your course once and then ignore the dashboard for the rest of the trip. You continuously monitor indicators like fuel level, engine temperature, and warning lights. You adjust your speed and direction based on road conditions and traffic. You refuel when the tank gets low.

Self-discovery works much the same way. The awareness and understanding you develop become your dashboard—not a one-time achievement but a continuous monitoring system that helps you navigate your life with greater consciousness and choice.

This system requires regular attention. You need to check in with yourself—your feelings, needs, boundaries, energy levels, and alignment with your values. You need to notice when your "tank" is running low and take steps to refuel. You need to watch for warning lights that signal misalignment or neglect of important aspects of yourself.

This ongoing attention isn't a burden or sign of failure. It's simply how the system is designed to work. Just as your car continuously consumes fuel and requires regular maintenance, your self-awareness requires consistent attention and care. There's always a "burn of gas," always a need to recharge your battery, always something to feed and maintain.

This reframing from destination to dashboard shifted Claire's relationship with self-discovery. Rather than feeling deflated that she hadn't "arrived" once and for all, she began to appreciate the tools and awareness she'd developed as valuable navigation instruments for the ongoing trip.

"I think I've been approaching this like a mountain to climb," she reflected. "Like once I reached the summit of self-knowledge, I'd be done with the hard part. But it's more like learning to sail, isn't it? You don't master sailing and then stop paying attention to the wind and waves. The mastery is in the ongoing responsiveness to conditions, both external and internal."

"That's a beautiful metaphor," I told her. "Yes, exactly that."

THE CERTAINTY TRAP

One of the most common obstacles to accepting the ongoing nature of self-discovery is called the "certainty trap"—our deep desire for definitive, unchanging answers about who we are and what we want.

This desire is understandable. Certainty feels safe. It promises relief from the anxiety of not knowing or the discomfort of change. If we could just figure ourselves out once and for all, we imagine, we could navigate life with confidence and clarity, free from doubt or confusion.

But this yearning for absolute certainty about ourselves is both unrealistic and ultimately limiting. We are not static entities but dynamic, evolving beings. Our preferences, capacities, values, and even identities shift and develop throughout our lives in response to new experiences, relationships, challenges, and insights.

Daniel, a client in his thirties, struggled particularly with this desire for certainty. A successful engineer who valued precision and definitive answers, he found the fluid nature of self-discovery profoundly unsettling.

"I just want to know, definitively, who I am and what I want," he told me in one session. "I feel like I should have this more figured out by now."

"What if certainty isn't the goal?" I suggested. "What if the goal is developing a relationship with yourself that can accommodate uncertainty, change, and ongoing discovery?"

Daniel looked genuinely perplexed. "But how do you make decisions without certainty? How do you know which path to take?"

"The same way you navigate any complex, evolving system," I offered. "Not with absolute certainty but with thoughtful attention to the information available in this moment, knowing you'll continue to gather more information as you go."

The alternative to the certainty trap isn't aimless drifting or indecision. It's a different kind of confidence—not the rigid confidence of "I have all the answers," but the more resilient confidence of "I trust my capacity to navigate uncertainty and learn as I go."

For Daniel, rather than trying to arrive at irrevocable conclusions about himself, he began to approach self-knowledge as an ongoing conversation with an evolving self.

"I'm starting to see that my discomfort with uncertainty has actually limited me," he reflected after several months of work. "I've been so focused on finding definitive answers that I haven't allowed myself to explore or evolve. It's like I've been trying to solve myself like an equation, when maybe I'm more like a garden—something that grows and changes in response to conditions and care."

Self-discovery is not about solving yourself once and for all, but about cultivating an ongoing relationship with yourself that allows for growth, change, and continuing revelation.

EMBRACING THE AWKWARD

"I still feel so awkward sometimes," Claire admitted during our final session. "Even with all the work we've done, there are moments when

I just don't know how to be myself around certain people or in certain situations. Is that ever going to go away completely?"

"Probably not," I said with a smile. "And that's actually okay."

"Really?" She looked skeptical. "Because it doesn't feel okay. It feels like I should have it all figured out by now."

"Let me ask you something," I said. "Do you know anyone who seems to have it all figured out? Someone who never experiences awkwardness or uncertainty about themselves or how to navigate life?"

Claire thought for a moment. "Well, my boss seems pretty confident all the time. And my friend Melissa always knows exactly what she wants and how to get it."

"And do you know either of them intimately? Have you seen them in their private moments of doubt or confusion?"

"No," Claire admitted. "I guess I only see the public version."

"Here's something I've learned after decades of sitting with people in their most vulnerable moments," I told her. "No one has it all figured out. Everyone experiences uncertainty, awkwardness, and moments of not knowing exactly who they are or how to be. The difference isn't between people who experience awkwardness and those who don't; it's between those who can acknowledge and embrace it versus those who are terrified of it and expend enormous energy trying to hide it."

This truth—that awkwardness is a universal human experience, not a personal failing—can be remarkably liberating. So many of us believe we should have outgrown awkwardness by adulthood, that confidence means never feeling uncertain or uncomfortable with ourselves or others. We see awkwardness as evidence that we're somehow failing at being fully realized humans.

But what if awkwardness isn't a bug but a feature of authentic living? What if those moments of not knowing exactly who we are or how to be, are actually doorways to further growth and discovery?

The etymology of the word "awkward" offers a clue to its value. It comes from the Old Norse "afugr," meaning "turned backward" or "facing the wrong way." Awkwardness arises when we're momentarily disoriented, when our habitual patterns of self and relationship are disrupted, when we're not sure which way to turn.

This disorientation, uncomfortable as it may be, creates the conditions for new discovery. It's only when our automatic patterns are interrupted that we have the opportunity to choose more consciously, to experiment with new ways of being, to expand our repertoire of self-expression and connection.

For Claire, embracing awkwardness meant recognizing it not as a failure of her self-discovery work, but as an integral part of the ongoing process, a signal that she was entering new territory or encountering edges of growth.

"I'm starting to see awkwardness differently," she told me. "Last week at this networking event, I felt that familiar discomfort rising—not knowing quite how to introduce myself or what to say about my work. In the past, I would have beaten myself up for still feeling this way after all our work together. But this time, I just thought, Oh, hello awkwardness, my old friend. You're letting me know this is a growth edge for me. And somehow, acknowledging it that way made it less overwhelming."

This shift—from fighting awkwardness to befriending it—represents a significant development in the expedition of self-discovery. It moves us from seeking a perfect, finished self who never experiences uncertainty to embracing a more authentic, evolving self who can navigate discomfort with curiosity rather than shame.

Another key aspect of accepting the ongoing nature of self-discovery is learning to hold the creative tension between structure and flow—between the frameworks, practices, and insights that provide stability and the openness to continuous evolution and discovery.

Throughout this book, we've explored various structures that support self-discovery: understanding your family patterns, mapping your relationship dynamics, clarifying your values, defining your own metrics, and building self-trust. These frameworks provide crucial scaffolding, offering orientation points and practical approaches for knowing yourself more deeply.

But these structures are meant to serve your ongoing discovery, not to constrain or finalize it. They're tools for navigation, not fixed destinations or irrevocable conclusions about who you are.

Mark, a philosophy professor in his early fifties, struggled with this tension between structure and flow in his approach to self-discovery. A naturally analytical person, he had diligently applied every framework and practice I suggested, creating elaborate systems for tracking his patterns, defining his values, and evaluating his choices.

"I've mapped everything out," he told me, showing me the detailed journal where he recorded his insights and observations. "I have my primary attachment style catalogued, my core values identified, and my relationship patterns documented. It's all here."

"That's impressive work," I acknowledged. "How is it serving you in your day-to-day life?"

Mark hesitated. "Well, that's the strange thing. Sometimes, all this analysis actually feels limiting rather than liberating. Like I've put myself in a box of my own creation."

With the popularity of assessments to help us know ourselves more at our fingertips, becoming confined by our own frameworks of self-understanding is common, especially for those with analytical minds. The structures that initially support our self-discovery can eventually become constraints if we relate to them as fixed and final rather than as evolving tools.

For Mark, the path forward involved holding these structures more lightly—using them as orientation points while remaining open to new discoveries that might not fit neatly into his existing frameworks.

"I'm learning that self-knowledge isn't just about analyzing and categorizing," he reflected several months later. "It's also about staying open to mystery, to the parts of myself I haven't yet recognized or understood. I still use the frameworks we've developed; they're incredibly valuable. But I hold them more provisionally now, as useful maps rather than perfect representations of the territory."

This balance between structure and flow, between the known and the unknown aspects of yourself, is at the heart of accepting the ongoing nature of self-discovery. The structures provide necessary orientation, but the flow allows for continuous growth and revelation.

THE PRACTICE

"Sometimes, I feel like I'm starting over," Kendal, a grade school teacher, confessed during one of our sessions. "I'll have this sense that I really understand myself, and then something happens—a conflict with my partner, a challenge at work, an unexpected emotional reaction—and suddenly, I feel like I'm back at square one, like all our work together hasn't made a difference."

"That feeling of starting over is actually part of the process," I assured her. "It doesn't mean you've failed or lost ground. It's more like a spiral than a linear progression: You keep circling back to similar themes but with greater awareness each time."

This experience of "beginning again" is familiar to anyone engaged in ongoing practices, whether meditation, creative work, athletic training, or self-discovery. Humility is required in acknowledging that we never completely transcend our basic challenges or patterns. Instead, we develop a more conscious relationship with them, approaching them with greater skill and compassion each time they arise.

In meditation traditions, this is sometimes called "the beginner's mind"—the willingness to approach each moment fresh, without being constrained by what you think you already know. In the context of self-discovery, it means remaining open to seeing yourself anew, even in areas where you believe you've already gained understanding.

For Kendal, embracing this practice of beginning again meant recognizing that moments of confusion or regression weren't failures but opportunities for deeper integration and discovery.

"I had this argument with my sister last weekend—the same old pattern we've been in since childhood," she told me. "For a moment, I felt completely discouraged, like all our work on my family dynamics hadn't made any difference. But then I realized something was different. I was able to notice the pattern while it was happening, to stay present with my reactions instead of just being consumed by them. I still got triggered, but I recovered more quickly and was able to repair the conversation instead of staying stuck in resentment for days."

Progress often looks like this growing capacity to navigate familiar patterns with greater awareness, resilience, and skillfulness. You must give yourself grace knowing that you may not eliminate your patterns once and for all, but you are developing a more conscious relationship with them over time.

The practice of beginning again asks us to approach ourselves with the same patience and persistence we would bring to any other meaningful discipline. Just as a musician doesn't practice an instrument once and expect mastery, or an athlete doesn't train for a week and expect peak performance, we don't engage in self-discovery work briefly and expect complete transformation.

Instead, we commit to the ongoing practice—returning again and again to the fundamental questions and challenges of knowing ourselves, each time with the benefit of greater experience and perspective.

"How do you keep doing this work year after year?" Kendal asked me during our final session. "Doesn't it get exhausting, constantly examining yourself and staying conscious of your patterns?"

It was a thoughtful question that went to the heart of sustaining the practice of self-discovery over a lifetime. Because Kendal was right—this work does require energy. Like driving a car, the exploration of knowing yourself involves a continuous "burn of gas," a steady consumption of attention and awareness that needs regular replenishment.

"You're absolutely right that it requires energy," I told her. "And like any ongoing endeavor, it's essential to develop practices that refuel you rather than just depleting your reserves. Self-discovery isn't meant to be a grinding exercise in self-improvement. At its best, it's a nourishing engagement with the mystery and wonder of your own being."

This perspective that self-discovery should ultimately be nourishing rather than depleting shifts how we approach the ongoing work. Instead of seeing it primarily as a disciplined effort we must force ourselves to maintain, we can recognize it as a fundamental form of self-care, a way of attending to ourselves that generates its own rewards.

Just as a car needs regular refueling to continue its trip, we need consistent practices that replenish our energy and attention for the ongoing work of knowing ourselves. These refueling practices will be different for each person, aligned with their unique temperament and circumstances, but they often include:

- **Connection With Others Who Support Authentic Self-Expression:** Few things are more nourishing than relationships where you can be genuinely seen and accepted. These connections provide both mirror and sanctuary—reflecting your authentic self back to you while creating safe space for exploration and growth.
- **Engagement With Nature, Art, or Spirituality:** Experiences that connect you to something larger than your individual concerns can provide essential perspective and renewal. Whether through time in natural settings, engagement with creative arts, or spiritual practices that resonate with you, these connections remind you that self-discovery isn't just about individual development but about finding your place in the larger web of life.

- **Physical Practices That Promote Embodied Awareness:** Movement disciplines like yoga, dance, tai chi, or mindful walking can help maintain connection with your body's wisdom, counterbalancing the tendency toward excessive mental analysis that can sometimes characterize self-discovery work.
- **Creative Expression That Allows for Exploration Without Judgment:** Creative practices—whether writing, music, visual arts, or other forms—offer valuable channels for self-discovery that bypass the rational mind's tendency to categorize and control. Through creative expression, aspects of yourself that might remain hidden in more analytical approaches can find voice and recognition.
- **Rest and Non-Doing:** Perhaps most counterculturally, genuine rest—time when you're not trying to achieve, improve, or even understand yourself—is essential for sustainable self-discovery. These fallow periods allow for integration and renewal, creating space for insights to emerge organically rather than being forced through constant effort.

Kendal discovered that while journaling felt like a chore, voice memos recorded during her morning walks provided a natural way to reflect on her experience. She found that certain friends consistently helped her reconnect with her authentic self, while others pulled her into performance or comparison. She learned that time in her garden offered both metaphor and medicine for her inner work—a living reminder of the cycles of growth, rest, and renewal that characterize all life processes, including self-discovery.

"I'm starting to see that this ongoing exploration doesn't have to feel like a burden," she reflected in one of our last sessions. "When I approach it with curiosity rather than pressure, when I include practices that genuinely feed me rather than just analyzing myself endlessly, it actually becomes energizing rather than depleting."

This shift from seeing self-discovery as a demanding discipline to recognizing it as a nourishing engagement with your own unfolding life is perhaps the most important foundation for sustaining the expedition over time. It transforms what might otherwise become another form of self-improvement pressure into a genuine practice of self-care and appreciation.

EMBRACING THE AWKWARD TOGETHER

One of the most liberating aspects of accepting the ongoing nature of self-discovery is recognizing that none of us have it all figured out. We're all navigating this human experience with varying degrees of consciousness, skill, and grace, but no one has achieved some perfect, finalized state of self-knowledge or self-mastery.

Understanding this universal truth can transform how we relate both to ourselves and to others. Instead of comparing our inner experience of uncertainty to others' outward appearance of confidence, we can recognize that everyone experiences moments of not knowing, of awkwardness, of wondering who they are and how to be.

This recognition creates the possibility for a different kind of connection—one based not on performing certainty or competence but on acknowledging our shared humanity, including the awkward, uncertain, evolving nature of being human.

"There was this moment at work last week," Kendal told me in our final session. "We were in this high-pressure meeting, everyone trying to sound authoritative and certain. And I just had this flash of insight—that everyone in that room, beneath their polished presentations, was dealing with some version of the same questions and doubts I experience. It suddenly seemed so absurd, all of us pretending to have everything figured out, when really we're all just figuring it out as we go."

"And how did that realization affect you?" I asked.

"It was like this wave of compassion, both for myself and for everyone else in the room. Instead of feeling like I was the only one who didn't have it all together, I could see our common humanity. And somehow, that made it easier to speak up authentically instead of performing confidence."

The shift from the isolation of believing everyone else has it figured out to the connection of recognizing our shared experiences creates the possibility for what I call "embracing the awkward together." It's a way of relating where we don't have to hide our uncertainty or pretend to have all the answers. Instead, we can acknowledge the ongoing nature of our becoming, creating space for authentic connection through our shared humanity rather than our performed perfection.

In practical terms, embracing the awkward together might look like:

- normalizing not-knowing in your conversations, using phrases like "I'm still figuring this out" or "I don't have a definitive answer yet"
- sharing your genuine process rather than just your conclusions, allowing others to witness your thinking and feeling in real time
- responding to others' vulnerability with appreciation rather than judgment, creating safe space for authentic expression
- approaching differences with curiosity rather than with defensiveness, recognizing that conflicting perspectives often reflect different stages or aspects of an evolving perspective
- finding humor in the universal human experience of awkwardness, not through mockery but through genuine appreciation for the endearing imperfection we all share

These practices don't eliminate the discomfort of uncertainty or the challenge of ongoing self-discovery. But they transform our relationship with these experiences from one of isolation and inadequacy to one of shared humanity and mutual support.

THE EXPEDITION CONTINUES

As we conclude our foundational exploration of self-discovery, I want to acknowledge both how far you've come and how much lies ahead. The insights, practices, and perspectives we've explored together provide valuable tools for knowing "Where am I in this?" and living more authentically. But they aren't the end point—they're provisions for an ongoing expedition of discovering your starting point on every path you walk.

Like Kendal, you may sometimes feel you've found "Where am I in this?", only to encounter situations that reveal new aspects of yourself or challenge your existing understanding. Like Daniel, you may yearn for certainty about who you are, only to discover that the living reality of your being is more fluid and dynamic than any fixed definition could capture. Like Mark, you may develop elaborate frameworks for understanding yourself, only to find that life continuously presents experiences that don't fit neatly into your existing categories.

These challenges aren't failures of your self-discovery process. They're inherent to the nature of being human—a complex, evolving being engaged in an ongoing dialogue with yourself, others, and the world around you.

The invitation of this book isn't to arrive at a final destination of understanding, but to develop a more conscious, curious, and com-passionate relationship with your ongoing discovery. It's an invitation to approach yourself not as a problem to solve once and for all, but as a mystery to engage with throughout your life—sometimes with clarity and confidence, sometimes with uncertainty and awkwardness, always with the potential for deeper discovery and authentic expression.

As you continue this path, remember that you don't need to have it all figured out to live with meaning and authenticity. You don't need perfect self-knowledge to make choices aligned with your values, to connect genuinely with others, to contribute your unique gifts to the world. You simply need the willingness to stay engaged with yourself: to keep checking your dashboard, refueling your tank, adjusting your course as needed, and embracing the beautiful, messy, ongoing process of discovering where you are and who you're becoming.

And perhaps most importantly, remember that you're not alone on this path. We're all navigating the same fundamental questions and challenges, all experiencing moments of clarity and moments of confusion, all figuring it out as we go. In that shared humanity lies the possibility for genuine connection, mutual support, and the joy of discovering ourselves together, awkwardness and all.

So here's to your self-discovery, to your finding "where you are in this," not as a race to some finish line of perfect self-knowledge, but as an ongoing adventure of discovery, growth, and authentic expression. May you approach it with curiosity rather than pressure, patience rather than perfection, and the deep trust that even in the moments when you feel most lost or confused, you're exactly where you need to be in the unfolding process of discovering more of the beautiful mystery that is you.

ABOUT THE AUTHOR

Dr. Lee Long, EdD, LPC-S, is an internationally respected therapist and clinical leader with nearly 30 years of experience helping people heal from depression, trauma, and emotional pain. As CEO of Restoration Counseling, he is known for blending clinical excellence with warmth, humor, and deeply relational care.

Learn more at DrLeeLong.com